My Four Friends

My Four Friends

◆

Growing up On A Northern Minnesota Farm

Joe McGraw

iUniverse, Inc.
New York Lincoln Shanghai

My Four Friends
Growing up On A Northern Minnesota Farm

Copyright © 2007 by William J. McGraw

iUniverse books may be ordered through booksellers or by contacting:

iUniverse
2021 Pine Lake Road, Suite 100
Lincoln, NE 68512
www.iuniverse.com
1-800-Authors (1-800-288-4677)

Because of the dynamic nature of the Internet, any Web addresses or links contained in this book may have changed since publication and may no longer be valid.

The views expressed in this work are solely those of the author and do not necessarily reflect the views of the publisher, and the publisher hereby disclaims any responsibility for them.

ISBN: 978-0-595-46237-7 (pbk)
ISBN: 978-0-595-70036-3 (cloth)
ISBN: 978-0-595-90538-6 (ebk)

Printed in the United States of America

For My Wife
Josephine McGraw
Who Has Done So Very Much For Me
And Who I Love Very Much

A House On Wheels

Could that be the rooster doing his usual morning celebration, singing his hello to the whole world? Yes, it certainly was! Time to get out of bed! Time to get down the stairs! Time to get outdoors! To me, mornings on the farm, with my Grandpa and all the animals, were always nice, especially to an almost five-year-old Joe McGraw.

Out of bed I jumped, into my clothes I got and out the door I bounded with not so much as a "Good Morning All". Outside, I see absolutely no one. I ran to the barn to see if Grandpa or Kieser were there. Nope, they aren't up and about yet. I went out the back door of the barn into the fenced pasture. I see no one at all. I walked around the pasture, taking my time, looking at all the trees with their big branches. Gee, I wondered if one of the branches was strong enough to hold me. Then I looked over at the small mound of a hill next to the fence by the railroad track to see if the woodchucks are awake. I didn't see any movement. I continued on my way, just kicking the grass and looking at the branches of the trees.

Soon I came by some fairly large poplar trees and I saw one with a branch that would possibly hold me. I walked all around the tree to decide. When at last I made up my mind that the branch in question would hold me, up to the tree I go, and began to climb up to the branch. After about an hour or so just sitting up there on the branch, I heard something from the direction of the roadway. As much as I tried I just couldn't make out what was making all the noise. Could it be some sort of new train? Could it be a lot of dump trucks hauling gravel? Could it be some strange, new kind of contraption that they hadn't told me about yet? I was at a loss to name the source of all the noise. I muttered under my breath, "What the heck was the noise all about?" I was beginning to feel really excited.

I cranked my head around to try to hear what the noise was all about. I looked toward the noise, but I couldn't see anything out of the ordinary. The birds were all in their trees singing. The dogs were still asleep on the grass; the cats were asleep on their porches. Still I heard the awful noise; I just couldn't make out what it was. I sat and listened to it for a little while, hoping to get a clue as to where it was coming from. Certainly it was not an animal of any sort. I let myself out of the tree and climbed down to the ground. I could hear it more plainly now.

I cautiously looked all around, with no luck at all. I bent over, down on one knee hoping to get a better view of the landscape around me, but not a glimpse did I get. There were too many trees to get a good look in any direction. The noise had escalated to the level of a din. It actually hurt my ears to listen to it. There has to be a way to get close enough to see it, I thought, and then I set off, on foot, in the direction of the noise. I soon found the going to be a little rough with the underbrush and tall grass. I stumbled at almost every step, that is, until I got near the roadway. Then the going got good enough for me to make a better headway.

The din had escalated to the level of a deep, clanking roar. It had a metallic sound to it, along with chuffing and clanking. It seemed to be just ahead of me now. Just a little further and soon I would be able to see it. What was that just ahead? Was that a chimney I was looking at? No, it couldn't be, not way up here on the roadway. There has never been a house out here. Besides, what would a chimney be doing out by itself in the middle of the road? That's hard to say. I just left it as it was and kept on making my way to the roadway. In about ten minutes or so, maybe even fifteen, I came upon the roadway.

Sure enough, I soon saw what the noise was all about. There on the roadway was a glimpse of something moving very, very slowly along. Could it be a truck? No, a truck doesn't make that kind of clanking noise. What could it be then? A few more yards and I could begin to see the roadway in the clear. There it was, making all the noise and clanking.

It was a caterpillar tractor of the 1920's era. I hadn't seen one of those in a long while, three years to be sure. Even the township had more modern equipment than that old tractor. I wondered where it came from and who was doing the driving. It's got to be some old duffer with a lot of time on his hands, that's for sure. Could be it was someone who Grandpa knew. He knew just about everybody in the surrounding area. Sure enough, it was the General from the world war. He was up on the seat of the tractor just having a ball.

Moving up closer to the roadway now, I could see that the tractor was pulling a house on wheels. It was a big house, at least two stories high with a large porch on one side. It was a nice looking house, but old. It looked as though no one had lived in it in quite a while. The paint was dull and weatherworn and hadn't been touched up for years and years. The windows all seemed to be in need of some putty, to say the least. The second story to the house seemed to be fairly small. It was just that, a second story. It didn't hold any promise at all.

The big question in my mind was "Where is this big house going?" It was coming on the trace headed for what seemed to be the farm. A trace is a pathway made by wagon teams. But why, certainly we had enough room with our little, two-room house. Could it be that someone had gotten the directions wrong and the house wasn't going to be on the farm? Could the house be headed for the other side of the valley? Is it possible that it is destined to be the house for the old woman above the far side of the valley? And just who were all these guys with the long poles walking along side the house. Why were they there anyhow? They had the tractor didn't they? And what's with all those long poles? All these questions were asked but not answered very readily, at least, not by me

The tractor, the house, all twenty guys came to a halt at the top of the trace leading to the farm. While they sat there resting, John Adams came up the trace with his team of horses. I was getting curious, more and more so by the minute. What the heck was John Adams doing up here with his team? Then up the slope came John Arco with his team, followed by Grandpa with his two teams of horses. If that doesn't beat all! Here were the three best horsemen in the valley with their teams of horses. What the devil was going on? Were they all just here to watch the house moving along? Boy, what a head scratcher this was turning out to be!

Right then the tractor started up again and moved the house and all to the lip of the hill on the trace. Grandpa, John Adams, and John Arco moved their teams to a position behind the house, and backed them up to about ten yards away. Each of them connected their teams to the long chains that were dragging behind the house. They then shouted "OK" to the tractor driver, and the whole shebang began to move down the hill of the trace.

The men took up their positions along the sides of the house with their poles, holding the house as steady as they could. The whole caravan moved ever so slowly on the down trace. The tractor, the house, the forty or so guys with the poles, and the four teams of horses were moving slowly down the hill. The poor horses didn't seem to know how to walk backwards. They were having a heck of a time.

Until, at last, the tractor and the house reached the bottom of the hill. For sure, this was a momentous arrival. The house was all in one piece and ready to be toted across the fields to its resting place. Angling to the Northeast was a roadway of sorts made of the gravel that Grandpa had put down during the month or two before the house was moved. Now all that remained to do was to do it. Without further ado, the tractor turned into the field with the house close behind. Making the turn at the field corner was a little tight, and the men had to take out another fence post to let the house pass.

At last, they were into the first field and started on the last half mile of their journey. All that remained was to get the house over the next bit of land in one piece and they would have it made. The gravel in the field wasn't a packed-down roadway as were all the roads they had traversed getting down this far. It was made up of loose gravel four to five inches deep. They still had a half-mile to go until they got to the site for the house to stand. "Let's get on with it then", shouted the gang boss.

The whole entourage began to move ever so slowly across the first field. Moving cautiously was the name of the game. The tractor sank into the loose gravel right off. The gang boss was very concerned and warned all the men to keep a sharp eye out for the house. No one wanted to have an accident at this point were especially concerned about having the house fall off the wheels.

It looked like another hour or two would be sufficient to cross the fields. All the men were getting a little tired about then, and the gang boss was even more vigilant than he had been. He kept walking around the tractor and the house, talking to the men as he did. "Hey, you guys", he exhorted, "pay attention to the house!"

Then suddenly the house shifted violently. "Lookout!", shouted one of the men. They stuck their poles up, trying to hold the house still and keeping it from shifting any further off the gravel roadway. As much as they tried to keep the house steady, it was rough going; especially since the house wheels weren't on solid ground. To make matters worse, water started to come up from the ground, getting the men's shoes wet. The water was coming from the swamp right close by and on a level with the gravel roadway that Grandpa had laid down.

They had moved only a half-mile in two and a half hours. The men could see the final destination but the tractor hadn't even started up the last hill. Just a little more effort and they would have it in place. Sure enough, only a couple of hours more was all that was needed to get the house up next to the future site of the foundation.

All the women were out on the hillside by then, standing in the field, urging their men along with hoots and hollering that could be heard even above the noise of the tractor. "That looks great, Jack", one of them shouted. Another said, "Look out for that bolder". Soon the tractor started up the last hill. There just ahead was the spot where the foundation was to be laid for the house. With just a little more effort they would reach it.

By now the men were getting a little tired and some of them lay down on the grass to rest. The rest of them kept on with their duties of guarding the house against falling off the wheels. It took almost an hour to position the house where it would be easy to put it on top of the walls of the basement. It was evening twilight before they got the house up there.

Now all that remained was to wall in the basement, put the house on the foundation, dig out the basement, set up a new furnace and heat lines and vents, dig a new well for the new water lines and hang the doors for the basement garage. Whew! What a lot of work that would be! Just who was going to do it all? That's really "all that remained?"

All that was well and good, but let's get some supper. We hadn't eaten all day and some of the men were beginning to gripe about it a little. "Hey, I'm about ready to eat a chicken", one guy said. Ah ha, the women folk were ahead of them on that score. They had all the makings of a fine dinner already cooked and on tables in the little house just waiting to be eaten.

The men let out a big hoot when their women called them to come and eat. Come they did! All the men, with all their women, and all their kids, came to the tables to help themselves to the food. Poor old Grandma just stood and watched and cried with a smile on her face as big as all get-out. She was happy because this was HER house. She had picked it out by herself and paid it for by herself. Grandpa put his arm around her shoulders and hugged her close. Neither of them said a word. They both stood there with the tears of joy falling down their faces.

"Time was a-wasting", as they say in the better circles. Here it was July already and that didn't leave much time to get the basement dug and the foundation set up. The men were talking about getting back before long to do just that. In fact, some of them were already volunteering for the next weekend. One of the men kidded Grandpa by saying "This is more fun than I've ever had!" But Grandpa said, "No, because I can't get the channels dug for the walls in so short a time."

All the men wanted to know when could he get the job done. Grandpa said, "I might be able to do the job in the next two weeks." At this, they all let out a hoot and a holler, and went back to their eating chores. The kids all jumped up and down with joy, because they'd get to come to the farm again in two weeks. Soon, dinner was done and the men took their plates to the stream for washing.

Four or five of the men chose to take a dip in the stream in their shorts. Some one said, "It's getting late. We'd better be off." Everybody got dressed and headed for their cars. Soon, they were just a cloud of dust on the road to town. Grandpa and Grandma stood there arm and arm watching the crowd disappear, enjoying the day, hoping the time would pass quickly so that they could move in to their new house.

On Monday morning, Grandpa was up early and started his chores milking and feeding the cattle. Almost at a run, he dashed back and forth carrying pails of milk to the house. Then he pumped water into the water tank. Using a pitchfork, he gave hay to the cattle.

When he finished with all his chores, he got the team out and hitched up the sand dredge. He drove the team over to the hill where the house was to be set on its new foundation. He parked the team at the bottom of the hill. He got out a measuring tape and went to the top of the hill. There he plotted out the basement walls and marked them.

Now that he had finished this job, he came back down the hill to get the team again. He drove the team up the hill to the top and began dredging the sand. He started in the Northwest corner and proceeded to go to the Southwest corner of the plat. He drove the team down to dump the dredge and returned to the top. This time though he dredged from the Northwest corner to the Northeast corner. He then came over to the dumping place and started to make a pile of sand. Going back again another time, he took the team and started to dredge from the Southwest corner to the southeast corner.

Now he had the perimeter marked out. All he had to do was to continue with the dredging until the digging was deep enough to build the walls of the basement. Unfortunately, the dig for the walls became too narrow for the team. Grandpa was forced to make a decision. Get rid of the team and use a single horse for dredging out the sand, or dig the rest of the way all by hand. As it happened, he did a little of each. He rigged up the dredge for a single horse and proceeded with the digging that way. This went on until Friday when he found the wall dredging again too narrow for even one horse. From about noon on Friday he started digging by hand. He kept this up until the job was finished, next Thursday evening.

Grandpa went to town to call all the men to come back out to the farm to work again. But it was a little bit different now. The men would have to be willing to work on the wall. With all of its responsibilities, this would be much different from walking the house along the roadway. Most of the men said, "OK, we'll be there", but one of them said, "I'm not sure that I'm up to the task." A few others chimed in with the same remark. Grandpa said, "Oh, this isn't anything that you all can't handle … you're all very good at what you do and you should be able to do it all right".

They all volunteered to be there on the next day. The women volunteered to do the cooking, and the kids were sure to be there, playing. Everything was beginning to look rosy. By this time next week the house would be sitting on its foundation fat and stone faced, while Grandma would have a happy smile on her face, to say the least.

It was Friday and at 7am Joe Monti, the cement maker, was on hand. He parked his truck out of the way, took out his sextant and came over to see how the walls were coming along. He said to Grandpa, "Wow! You sure have made a lot of progress from the last time I was here." Grandpa and Grandpa just beamed from ear to ear without a word. Then Monti went over to his truck and unhitched the cement maker. He took it by hand over to the pile of sand that Grandpa had made from digging out the channels for the wall.

Monti said, "OK, everything is ready". Shortly, the men started to arrive. They came across the field where they had been just two weeks ago when they were escorting the house. Along with them was a man that no one knew. No one that is, but Joe Monti. Joe Monti went over to this guy and started a conversation with him. They talked like long lost buddies for fifteen minutes or so. We couldn't quite make out the words, but were still curious as to who he was.

Monti gave a little talk to the men about laying cement for a wall. They all listened to his every word about how to lay cement. Pairing them off into teams of two, Joe Monti assigned them to positions on the wall. "You boys …" Mr. Monti said, "you are getting big enough to help. So, you two carry these pails and fetch water from the creek for the cement mixer." What a job that turned out to be. We had two pails apiece and were kept running back and forth to the creek to keep them full of water for the mixer. Monti kept mixing the cement, we kept bringing the water for the mixer and before we knew it, it was noon and we were dead tired. The women were calling all of us to dinner. What a good break that made.

The men showed up scraping the cement off their pants. Grandma had Auntie Dora bring down about a dozen chickens that she had cooked during the night before. The women had also fixed many salads, bread and deserts. Dad got out the seven cases of beer that he had brought that morning from the popshop. The popshop was a place where soda pop was manufactured.

All the kids were not left out of the festivities. Dad had brought along several cases of pop, which he opened up for the kids. Everyone ate and drank his fill. Without any further ado, the men all got up from the table and went back to work. They had the whole afternoon to complain as much as they wanted to, and complain they did, all in a joking sort of way, of course. One guy said, "I didn't eat enough to work this hard!" Monti just kept on sending them the cement and they just kept on building the walls.

Monti's friend, the stranger, kept walking around, looking at the men and wondering what they were doing. He kept his sextant in close range, taking sightings with it every now and then. After one of these sightings, Grandpa went over to Monti and asked who the guy was. Monti made all kinds apologies for not introducing him in the first place. Then he took Grandpa over to the place where the man was standing and introduced him as the State Road Inspector. After that, all were happy, and the work went on. There weren't any more furtive looks sent his way by the men who were also wondering about the guy. Now everyone was happy and all smiley as they continued on with their work.

It began to look as though the day was nearly done. The women called for the men to come and eat their supper, which they all did. Monti walked around the walls of the foundation to see for himself just how much work that was yet to be done. Then he came in and ate his supper too.

After supper, Monti stood up and clanked his glass to get the attention of everyone. When everyone was watching and listening, he made the announcement that they were all here for the night. This made for a lot of long faces in the crowd. No one was pleased with this turn of events. Monti went on to explain the reasons for his news. He said that everyone could leave, but that they were to expect to be right back here in two or three years doing the same job all over again from the beginning under much harder circumstances than now. The reason was the walls would start to crumble within a year unless they were finished properly now.

When the men heard that, they decided to go right back to work after they had finished their meal. "Gee", I thought to myself, "I don't know what was wrong, but the men considered it important." It only took a couple of minutes to finish off the meal. Then they all got up and went back to work. In another couple of hours Monti took a walk around the foundation and nodded his head in satisfaction. The State Road Inspector sighted each wall with the sextant, indicated that he also liked the foundation walls.

Monti began to worry about the gas for the cement maker. Would the couple or three gallons that he had left be enough to make enough cement for the foundation to be finished? Or would he have to get in his car and go get some more? He decided that he would have enough and continued on making cement. In any case he didn't have to worry because the State Road Inspector got into Monti's car and drove off to get some more gas.

Soon, he was back, just as the cement maker ran out of gas. He drove right up to the cement maker and stopped. When he got out of the car and said that he had gotten enough gas, everybody let out a big cheer. They were all as happy as can be. Now it would be just another hour and the job would be done. That was just about what it took to finish the walls.

The men started getting down from their perches and were getting cleaned up a little. The women were anxious to get moving. The kids were tired and wanted to go home to their beds. Then Monti got up on a chair and said thank you to them, inviting everyone to come back for an outing before the snow flew. They all packed into their cars and were ready to go.

Grandpa and Grandma were smiling as much as could be while giving thanks to the State Road Inspector and to Monti for their work. Here was another day of fine work done by the men and women, and don't forget about their children too.

Smiling, the two of them stood looking at the house and wondering just when it would be set onto the foundation. How could Grandpa do it all alone? I guess we'd just have to wait and see about that.

I got up about 5:00 am the next morning and immediately went outside to see the new house in the clear daylight of dawn. Sure enough, it was exactly where we had left it the previous evening. It was sitting there on the wheels by the foundation walls just waiting to be set down on its moorings. But that wouldn't be for a while, at least not until Grandpa figured how to set it on the foundation walls. That was the stickler in the mess. Just how was he going to do that anyway? We'd have to wait until next week and maybe later to see what means he would use. In the meantime today was Saturday! Hooray! Hooray

Grandpa Went To Town

Saturday was the best day of the week, bar none! Saturday was the day that Grandpa went from the farm into town, an 8-mile drive. Ronnie and I lived in town above the grocery store where we were waiting for him. We lived above the store with many other family members. It was also the best day because we got to go with him on his rounds in town. Sometimes we got to go other places, but these Saturday outings were the most fun. We always got to go everywhere with whoever was going at the moment, be it Grandpa, Dora or Dad—or even my mother, when she would consent to drive the car.

To say the least though, Saturday was Saturday. Oh Man! Oh Man! Oh Man! We were ready! We stood at the top of the stairway waiting for Grandpa to get into his Sunday best and to head out into town. When, at last he came out of the bedroom, he said his usual "Let's go boys!" to the empty stair top. We were way ahead of him, at the foot of the stairs, waiting to do just that: GO! Then he saw us standing there, waiting for him, so he came as quickly as he could to meet us. On his arrival at the bottom of the staircase, he again said, "Let's go boys", and headed for the Chevy coupe.

There was no holding us back. We took off through the store, the back room, out to the garage, and into the coupe barely touching the seat of the coupe and waited for Grandpa to come out. We were so excited that we felt like we were almost floating above the seat. Grandpa came out to the garage, got inside, started the car, and backed it out of the garage. Before we had a chance to ask he said,

"We are going to the barber shop. We are all three going to get a hair cut."

Wow! What a day this was turning out to be! We hadn't had a haircut since Christmas week, and were looking pretty shabby. We stood up on the car seat so we could see and be seen by all our friends in the neighborhood as we went by. Down the street we went, past the Lincoln school and the adjacent baseball field. We turned left at the Third Avenue corner and drove up the little hill on our way to Roseske's Barber Shop. At Railroad Street we turned right and then parked in front of the Barber Shop. "Let's go," said Grandpa. Out of the car we climbed and went into the barbershop.

Mr. Roseske was indeed glad to see us. He took one look and said, "You boys should come in more often. You look like you could really use a good, clean haircut. You've got hair as long as any I've seen this summer, longer even." With that he sat me up in the barber chair, and then he decided that I would need a booster board. He went to get the board and came right back. Then he sat me down on the booster board and said, "What kind of a haircut do you want?" When Grandpa didn't say any thing, I piped up with "I'd like a butch cut, please." "OK" says Mr. Roseske and he started in on my head just cutting away for all he was worth.

After about a few minutes he spun me around to face the mirror and said, "Now how does that look?" To me it looked fine, but for some reason, I said, "Make it a little shorter, please." He proceeded to do just that, trimming the top so it would stand up better. Then he said, "OK, you're all done." I climbed out of the chair and went over to where Grandpa was sitting so that he could get a good look at me. He did look me over quite well, and let out a stifled sigh of pain when he took a good look at me. He only said, "Your mother isn't going to like this."

Then it was Ronnie's turn to get up in the chair. Which he did, then he said to Mr. Roseske, "I would like a haircut like the one you gave Joey." Ronnie got a butch haircut too. The two of us were in for a lot of trouble when our mothers got sight of us. That wasn't going to be for another three or four hours yet so we might as well enjoy ourselves. That's exactly what we did while Grandpa was getting his haircut and a shave.

Ronnie got into the extra chair and I gave him a good shove to spin the chair around and let him come to a complete stop before I gave him another shove. Then Ronnie said that I should get in the chair. I did just that. Then he gave me a hard spin and said, "I think I can spin you faster". We spun each other around like this for about an hour and a half while Grandpa was getting all dolled up with a shave and a haircut. Soon, it was time to go. We ran out to the coupe and got in the rumble seat. Grandpa settled into the driver's seat and started the car.

We left the Barber Shop and went for the usual ride down to Washington Street and over the hill to the Boeing Location where many of our friends lived. It was good to see Joey Schiponi and his two cousins that had just arrived from Italy. Geno and Dario were sort of glad to see us, because we spoke Italian almost as well as they did. But we wouldn't speak the language to them because they were supposed to be learning English while they were playing around with other kids. After a short visit, Grandpa said, "Let's go boys". With that we got back in the rumble seat ready for anything that was offered to us. The two cousins wanted to go along with us, but we had to say no. It would be too far across town and there were too many hills for them to climb, and it would be too far for them to walk back alone.

The next stop was at Petronis' house, where we found Jim and his mother out in the yard. We stopped and visited with them for a little while. Jimmy was a quiet kid without too much to say, that is until he was asked to say something then you had better lookout. He could speak with the best of them, bar none. Jimmy proved that on this day and talked for an hour or more. After a short visit, Grandpa said,

"Let's go home, boys." With that we jumped into the rumble seat, Grandpa got in the driver's seat and off we went up the McKinley Street hill toward the store. When we got even with the courthouse, we were stopped by one of the guards who had been watching out for us.

The guard wanted to know when the food that had been ordered on the previous afternoon would be delivered. Of course, Grandpa didn't have any way of knowing about the order, so he said that as soon as he got back to the store, he would find out about the food. He started to drive off, when Doris Amis came rushing out to the car screaming her head off. We were all aflutter with that and grandpa stopped the car again. Doris rushed up to him and said that her mother had fainted on the kitchen floor and could we come and take her to the hospital.

Now, that was a real turn of events. Grandpa got out of the car and he and the guard went up to the Amis house. That left Ronnie and I there on the street wondering what we should do, and we were forced to wait right there for Grandpa to come back. Pretty soon he did do just that. He came running over to the car and said "You boys know how to get to the store from here, don't you?" We said "Sure we do Grandpa."

With that he said that we would have to walk back to the store, and for us to get out of the car. This we did without any delay and he started the car and took off for the Amis house. We went down to the corner where we could watch a little better and sat down on the grass. Pretty soon Grandpa and the guard came down the back steps carrying Mrs. Amis and put her in the car. We decided to go back to the store while Grandpa drove off toward the hospital.

In about a half an hour we got back to the store. Boy did we get all the funny looks! "Where did we leave Grandpa? Wasn't he coming back?" both Ada and Dora wanted to know. We told them about Mrs. Amis and how Grandpa was taking her to the hospital. You'd think that started a fire in the building, the women were running around hollering their heads off.

Mary, Ronnie's mother, and my mother came down the stairs lickety split and joined in the conversation. Even Grandma came over to the group and put her two-cents-worth in. All of them were so absorbed in the emergency and the missing Grandpa that none of them, not one, noticed our haircuts. Ronnie and I went upstairs to try to find some lunch. Our mothers came up shortly and, amid other things, they gave us some lunch. Then they wanted to know where we had been.

We told them all about the barbershop without mentioning our haircuts. Then all of a sudden Mary let out a scream. Then she said, "Where is all your nice hair?" That started the two of them off on a nonstop trip to the hot place for sure. I had to admit that I had gotten the first haircut and the barber just assumed that Ronnie wanted the same kind of cut. That little fib got poor Ronnie out of the hot water for the time being anyhow. We both let out a sigh of relief and then Grandpa came home and came up stairs.

The women were all aflutter asking just what had happened to poor Mrs. Amis. Grandpa, in fine Italian style, began to tell everyone about the whole incident, leaving out not a detail. Again, all this was all done in fine Italian style to say the least. Poor Mrs. Amis had gotten up at the usual time of 5:00 o'clock am and gotten her husband off to his work. She sat down to have some breakfast, after which she went into the living room to listen to the radio for a while. That was all she could remember. The doctor thought that she was pregnant again. Doris had said that her mother would never do that again, whatever "that" might have been. I guess little boys weren't supposed to hear about "that" at all. We just went down stairs and outside to play. And play we did for the rest of the day until supper time when the women came outside too get us to come in and eat.

After supper, we went outside again to play and found that some of our friends from around the neighborhood were out playing too. They all wanted to know what we had done during the day so far. We told them about the barbershop and going over to the Boeing Location and about Mrs. Amis. We told them about what Doris had said, not quite sure whatever it really meant. Some of the older boys kind of laughed about that and we were just as bewildered as ever. We had no idea at all what Doris was talking about and said so to the boys. This got some funny chuckles out of some of them to say the least. They said only for us to sit down in the grass. That was our first introduction to sex. To be generous, we just said, "Oh." That was the end of it. It started to get dark out. Before too long we said, "good night" to the boys and started across the street for the store.

Sunday morning we went to church and then stuck around the store for most of the day. About five o'clock my father said, "Would you like a ride to the farm?" We, of course, were jumping up and down with excitement, and shouted, "Sure we would." With that little bit of fun out of the way, we ran for the stairway and galloped down to the car. Dad came down too in a little bit, and as soon as my mother came, we were off to the farm. We got the usual lecture on "No mischievous antics" as the order of the day all the way down to the farm. A light was on in the little house when we got there, so we just took our stuff in and said Hi to Grandpa who was sitting with Keiser reading the Italian Paper. Grandpa went out to say hello to my Mom and Dad, and before we knew it, they took off and headed back to town.

Monday we had deliveries to make in town. Grandpa said, "Let's go, boys." We jumped into the car and were on our way down to the cutoff to the Dupont Road. It was only about eight or nine miles to town that way. The road was straight as an arrow and mostly paved with oil and gravel. It was done that way for the Dupont Company trucks loaded up with dynamite on their way to the Iron Ore Mines by Hibbing and along the range. Before we had gone a couple of miles, Grandpa said, "We got to stop at Battleaxe's farm." and he turned in at the driveway. Why we wondered at the time, would anyone want a name like "Battleaxe" anyway. When we got up to the house we could see why he got the name of Battleaxe. He was just a plain ugly guy. We stayed there for a few minutes while Grandpa talked to Battleaxe. When he had done that, he got back in the car and off we went again.

We got another mile or two down the road and Grandpa said, "I wonder if Snootful is home." We turned into his driveway to go see if Snootful was indeed home. Sure enough, he was at home, just waiting for us to come up the driveway it seems. Grandpa drove up to the house and then old Snootful came out to meet us. Boy, he even looked like he had a snootful of something alcoholic. I guess that's how he got the name to start with, but you couldn't smell a thing on him. Grandpa said later that old Snootful just looked like that all the time. It took them about a half an hour to get their talking done and then off we went again this time for town for sure. I've got to be truthful with you, neither old Battleaxe nor old Snootful were drinkers at all. They were strictly sober gentlemen, and wouldn't take a drink of any thing even on Christmas Day.

Grandpa headed up the hill to go to the store and we were whistling through Park Addition, when all of a sudden an old lady stepped off the curb in front of us. Grandpa slammed on the brakes and managed to get stopped right beside her. She let out a scream that would wake the dead in the Third Avenue Cemetery. Thankfully she wasn't hurt at all, she wasn't even hit by the car, but we had had an awful scare.

All of us, including Grandpa, had been scared out of a year's growth. Grandpa got out of the car and went to see the little old lady in front of the car. He asked her if she had been hit. She said, "No, I am all right. But would you help me over to the car so I can sit down on the running board?" Grandpa was so shook up that he said, "Please get in the car," and he took her arm and pretty much pulled her along to the car door. Ronnie and I got in the back Rumble Seat and just sat down. Grandpa got her into the car, got in himself, started the car and started driving up to North Hibbing headed for the hospital. When we got there he jumped out of the car and said to the little old lady, "Come on. We're going in." She looked at him with a disgusting eye, but she dutifully got out of the car. Then Grandpa took her inside. He told the nurse that he had hit her with the car and would she please have the doctor examine her. The doctor did just that including an X-ray of her hip.

When he got done the doctor asked her when she had fallen. She said that she had fallen almost a year ago and that she had been awful sore afterward for a couple of months. The doctor said that he wasn't surprised seeing as how she had a broken hip at the time but there was nothing new that was broken and she could go home. With that Grandpa said, "Let's go," and we all went out to the car. The first stop was at the store to let us off. Here Grandpa had to explain why he had this old lady in the car with him. With that explanation Grandma came out to the car to visit. Wouldn't you know it, but it turns out that she knew the lady quite well. The two of them had quite a visiting session, about an hour or so. Then Grandma invited her into the store, and she went in just like she belonged there. Come to find out, she and Grandma were old friends and each enjoyed the company of the other.

That was all well and good, but Grandpa was getting antsy to get back to the farm. After a quick lunch, we climbed into the car again and started out for the farm. Down the Brooklyn road we went and we got on the highway to drive out of town. When we got to the county road going east from the highway and turned right to take it to the highway that came from Chisholm to Buddy's Tavern.

We were going along just fine until we got to the bridge construction over the river going through Mohka's farm. There we found the road all torn up. The county men were building a new bridge across the creek that ran through Mohka's farm. We had to stop and look around for another place to get across. Ronnie said that we should go north on the Spudville Road to the Kitsville Road and use that road to get to the highway into Wilpen. Then we could get ourselves back on this county road to get to the farm that way. That made sense. Off we went going on the Spudville Road.

Pretty soon we came upon the next road, but we couldn't tell if it was the Kitsville Road or not, but we took it anyway. We drove about five miles and there was another road that we couldn't tell if it was the Kitsville Road or not. We had spent a lot of time on the way to the farm today, and it was getting late for Grandpa's evening chores. He was getting a little anxious and said so, then I piped up with "Turn right, Grandpa", so he did. We drove along another five or six miles and we came to the Cutoff Highway from Chisholm to Buddy's Tavern. Grandpa knew he had to turn right again to get back to Wilpen. He did so and off we went again. Gee! It was six or six thirty by then and we could just hear the cows bellowing to be milked so we had to hurry it up a little bit.

Grandpa got the Chevy going along at a good clip and in almost no time we were back to Wilpen again. That little detour cost us about fifteen or twenty miles to say the least. It couldn't be helped with Mohka's bridge being out and all. So, when we got down from the bridge over the railroad track and turned left we were only about three miles from the farm. We could practically see it from here. At least we could see all the bad spots that the house had to be taken through getting it down to the farm.

Grandpa said that he was happy about the house, and that nothing had gone wrong with the house on the trip down. He could see where the guys with the long poles had gotten up next to it and held it up while going through the bad spots in the trace. All it would have taken was one wrong step, and the whole kit and caboodle would have gone over for sure. The house would have fallen off the wheels and the tractor would not have been able to stop it.

Soon we were at the farm. Grandpa got out of the car and made a run for the barn to begin his milking chore. We jumped out of the car too, but we didn't run. We merely trotted to the chicken coop and started our chores.

Scrubbing Chicken Eggs

The chickens seemed happy to see us. They all strutted around making little clucking noises and fluttered down from the rafters. They all crowded around us and seemed genuinely glad to see us. That was strange, indeed.

We first got the new straw in for their nests and then went out to the feed shed to get their feed out. When we first headed out to the feed shed, they all got lined up next to the door and waited for us to come back in. When we came in with the feed, they all started clucking away like forgotten kids to let us know that they were hungry. While we were dishing out the feed, Ronnie even had one chicken sitting on his shoulder waiting to be fed. When we got done with the feed we went to each nest and collected all the eggs. Turns out that there were quite a few eggs. The birds must have been working overtime or something. We put some of the eggs in our pockets and carried as many as we could, taking them back to the house for cleaning.

Then we came back for a second load of eggs. When we got back to the house the second time, we counted four dozen eggs. We pumped up two bowls of fresh water and set ourselves down to do the egg cleaning. This little chore took up about two hours. It only took us that long because the cleaning had to be done with cold water and a small brush. Following the cleaning job, we had to put all the eggs into cartons. This little chore took us until just about super time. When Grandpa said for us to come and get something to eat, we dropped all our tools, got cleaned up in no time and sat us down at the table.

While we were eating, Grandpa said, "Can you think of a way to clean the egg shells so it wouldn't take you so long to clean up a batch of eggs everyday?" "Sure," we said. "Just don't clean them so much each time we got a batch." We said. "No you can't do that kind of thing. The eggs have got to be clean for Grandma in the store every day." Grandpa replied. "Well we don't know of a way," we said together. "How does Mr. Pauley do his eggs, Grandpa? Maybe you should ask him to find out what the answer is." Grandpa replied, "But he lives way out south of South Hibbing. I can't be running all over the country to find an answer." he said.

We thought and thought about the problem more and more the longer we sat at the table. "We could try hot water and soap," we said. Then Ronnie said that we couldn't use hot water because we would wind up cooking the eggs and we couldn't do that. Ronnie said we could try wearing some large wool gloves or mittens. Then we would scrub the eggs with them. We decided that we couldn't do that either because we would shake up the eggs too much and possibly break the yokes in the eggs and maybe even break the shells of some of them.

There's just got to be another way I said, but what is it? We tried and tried to think of another way to clean the eggs but we just couldn't come up with a better way. As much as we tried to think of a better way, we just couldn't seem to come up with one. Until one day I happened to be scrubbing my teeth with the toothbrush and some toothpaste when it dawned on me, why don't we use the toothbrush on the eggs that would be a big help to brush the eggs when cleaning them?

I thought about it for the rest of the day and into the evening. The more I thought about it, the better the idea seemed to be. But first I had to get a couple of heavy-duty toothbrushes and an ample supply of toothpaste. So I broached the idea to Grandpa and he was all in favor of it. He said first thing we got to do is get hold of a toothbrush and some toothpaste, then we can sit down and try out the tools. I was pretty excited to say the least. Grandpa thought that my idea was good enough to give a try.

So the very next day found us on our way to town to find the necessary equipment. We went to drugstore after drugstore and looked at all the brushes that they had. None of them carried the heavy-duty type of brush and they all thought my idea was kind of half-baked. I'll show them just you wait and see. Then I got the idea that we should be visiting the Dentists office to see about getting the right kind of toothbrush. So our next visit was to Dr Kozrk up stairs of the Woolworth store.

Dr Kozrk wasn't too happy to see us since we weren't his patients, but he did the very best he could in listening to our proposal. When we had finished with our talk about cleaning up the eggs he said, "I've just the thing that you are looking for. Just a minute and I'll get it for you." So off he goes into the dentist's chair room and gets back in about ten minutes. In his hands there is a small black brush with a rather long handle. It looked like it could do the job real good, perhaps even too good. So we said we'd try it out and could he recommend toothpaste. He went ahead and gave us a list of all the toothpastes there were.

We decided to give the brush a try and got into the coupe and started off for the farm again. When we got to the top of the hill on the trace looking out over the valley where the farm was, we stopped to look at some deer in the woods just off to the side of the road. There were three of them just standing there watching us go by. They just stood there and looked at us as we were looking at them. I guess that we could have kept it all day, but other things were waiting to be done too.

So off we went again, down the trace to the gate of the farm. I got out of the car and opened the gate for Grandpa to drive through and to close the gate after he had driven through. When we got to the buildings area again Grandpa said it was lunchtime and promptly started making our lunch. I got the silverware and the plates out and set the table. When every thing was ready we sat down to eat our lunch. Boy did we eat! Everything that was in sight on the table was gone and we got up from the table with another good meal under our belts.

We decided that the chicken coop chores needed doing and went outside to go to the chicken coop. When we got there we found that the chickens were all up on the rafters and couldn't figure out why. So we went out to get some more straw for the nests and then started in collecting the eggs. In all there were quite a few of them, so we loaded up our pockets and arms with the first batch and headed out for the little house. We left all the eggs and headed back to the chicken coop to get the rest of the eggs for the day.

After going back to the chicken coop for the third time today, we were tired from all our running back and forth. Just as we got up to the coop we saw something just for an instant, and then it was gone again. The chickens were all up on the rafters and cackling away for all they were worth. We couldn't see why they were all so noisy and they went on with their cackling until we had brought in their feed and new straw for the nests. Then they finally settled down to peaceful quietude for a while. We left the coop then and went back over to the little house to begin cleaning today's batch of eggs.

When we got over to the little house we counted up six and a half dozen eggs. Boy! This cleaning job would take is all night! So we sat down and started in cleaning with the new toothbrush and some toothpaste. Sure enough the new brush was just what the doctor ordered, it did a wonderful job of cleaning the eggs just as if it had been made for the job. We'd have to remember to say thanks to the dentist who had given it to us.

The next day we were up bright and early and headed to the chicken coop to see if all the birds were all right. They all seemed to be OK when we got over to see them, so we decided to go for a walk up to John Arcos place. In going past the chicken coop we spotted what looked like a rat just leaving the coop itself. We didn't have the 22 with us so we were at a loss as to what to do. It didn't matter any way because the rat, or whatever he was, was long gone up the hill to the old farmhouse that had burned down a few years before. Wouldn't you know it but there were also some crows along the way just asking to be shot. Why weren't those old crows right around where we could shoot them when we had the 22 with us? I didn't know then, I don't know now, and I never will know.

We just took our time getting back to the farm and as luck would have it we were on time for our lunch. Grandpa was just finishing up making our lunch. I got out the silverware and the plates and set the table and we all sat down to eat. Ronnie and I were all ready to use the new brush on the eggs just as soon as we could. Right after lunch I had the dishes to do so I did them up and put them away. Then it was time to go to the chicken coop and start in on the chores there. Off we went to the chicken coop.

We got outside he door to the little house and remembered that we were going to bring the 22 with us. Back into the little house we went to get the 22 and some shells. Then we were ready to start out again. Start out we did going over to the chicken coop straight away. On the way over to the coop we didn't see the animal again. So much the better we could get on with our chores as soon as we got there.

We got the feed out for the chickens and then got the new straw in for the nests. After that we could start in picking up the eggs. We got our pockets and arms full and started out for the little house. When we had gotten to the little house it was getting toward 2:00pm and we hurried back for the rest of the eggs. We had gotten over to the coop just in time to see a rat or something running out of the coop and up the hill to the old house foundation. We had left the 22 in the coop for our run to the little house with the first batch of eggs.

We went into the coop and got the second load of eggs and still didn't have room to carry the 22. We had to leave it again. Over to the little house we ran and deposited our load of eggs and the back to the coop again to get the 22. Such a lot of running was enough to make me tired as could be. I just sat down outside the coop for a minute's rest, and then we were up and at them again, going back over to the little house to clean up this batch of eggs. We couldn't wait to try out the new brush again on the eggs.

When we had gotten over to the little house we pumped up two bowls of water, got the toothpaste, and the new brush, and sat down to clean the eggs. As soon as we tried the new brush we found that it didn't work as well at all. It was too stiff and scratched the eggs up real well. What the heck was wrong with the brush? It worked well yesterday when we used it. We were at a loss to figure out why the darned thing didn't do a well today. We tried it out brushing the eggs softly and didn't do any good at all, then we tried brushing the eggs hard and that didn't seem to do the trick either. We cracked an egg with all our brushing and we quit right there.

We hadn't gotten even a couple of eggs clean and here we were with all the eggs from today to get clean. What were we to do? So we decided to tell Grandpa about the brush as soon as he came in. In the meantime we went back to the old system of using an old small toothbrush and working a little harder at brushing the eggs to clean them up good enough for the store. Darn it anyhow. We were counting on that brush to do the job and now it was just too stiff for the job. We were disappointed to say the least.

When Grandpa came in about four o'clock we started in telling him about the brush and he said that we must be mistaken. So he picked up the brush and started to clean an egg. He had gotten about halfway done when the egg he was working on cracked. He had a very surprised look on his face, and he said, "What the heck! This egg cracked. I guess you boys were right about the brush; we'll have to give that dentist heck about the brush, and ask him why the brush was so hard to use." Then he said, "Have you finished up cleaning all the eggs today? If you have, put them into cartons and take them down to the basement. Then we will get our supper together."

As soon as we had done that "little" chore of putting the eggs into the cartons, we took them down to the basement where it was a little cooler. We had gotten several dozen eggs in cartons just waiting to be taken to town to the store. We told Grandpa how many dozen eggs we had ready and he said that were going to take them into the store tomorrow morning. Another week had gone by without our really knowing it.

In the morning we were up early by five am and did our morning chores before breakfast, and soon enough we were ready to go to town. We got all the eggs from the basement and had them ready to put in the car. Pretty quick Grandpa was done with his morning chores and we got the car loaded up with the eggs. Grandpa wanted to know if we had taken the new brush with us. Oh! My gosh! We had forgotten to put the brush into the car and had to run and get it. We were soon back and Grandpa said, "Andiamo." We were off like the wisp of smoke on a windy day.

We took the Dupont road going to town today just to look around a little I guess. When we got to town we had to drive down Howard Street to 3rd Avenue and then go up 3rd Avenue to Hibbing and Lincoln Street and to the store. When we got up to the store we had to unload all the cartons of eggs that we had brought along for the store. This took us about an hour while Grandpa was upstairs getting his bath taken. Pretty soon Grandpa was ready and off we went for the barbershop.

When we were done at the barbershop we got back in the coupe and started off for the dentist's office where we had gotten the brush.

When we got there we found that the Dentist's office was closed until Monday. We said, "What are we going to do now?" I said, "Lets go to Gambucis Hardware store. Maybe he'll have something we could use." So down to Brooklyn we went. We pulled up in front of the store at the gas pump and got out of the coupe.

We went into the store and Grandpa said that he needed some gas. Mr. Gambuci went out to pump the gas for us and we looked around the store. We didn't find anything that even looked like it could do the job of cleaning the eggs. Then Mr. Gambuci said, "Why don't you use a soft paint brush?" We were dumbfounded. Why hadn't we thought of that? Mr. Gambuci took us over to the paint counter and showed us some paintbrushes that we could possibly use. One in particular seemed to be about the right size and it was soft enough to do the job, we thought.

We bought the brush and went out to get back in the coupe. When we were all set to go Grandpa wanted to know if we were satisfied with the paintbrush, and we said that we could only give it an honest try. So back up to Hibbing we drove getting there just in time for lunch. After lunch we got ready to go back to the farm to try out the new brush. As soon as we were going again, we started to sing a happy song because we had gotten a good brush to try to clean the eggs with. We were ready to give it an honest try that afternoon when we got back to the farm.

At the farm we went immediately over to the chicken coop to begin our chores. We took the 22 with us too, and Ronnie was carrying it and some shells for it. When we got near the chicken coop we again saw the strange animal coming out of the wall in the coop. Ronnie took a shot at him, but he missed and the animal kept going up the hill by the burned out foundation.

We went into the chicken coop and there were all the chickens up on the rafters. When they saw us they began coming down and soon were all down on the floor. We got them their feed and new straw and then began to collect the eggs. We got our pockets full of eggs and our arms full too. We left the 22 there and walked over to the little house to leave the eggs. Then we went back over to the coop for a second load of eggs. It seemed like there were so many eggs that we couldn't carry them all. So we took that batch of eggs over to the little house and then came back for a third load of eggs and the 22.

We were anxious to try the new brush on the eggs and went right back to the little house to do just that. We pumped up two bowls of water and got the toothpaste out and ready. Then we sat down at the table and started in cleaning the latest batch of eggs. The brush seemed to work just fine. It did the cleaning job as good as we expected, even better. The only trouble was that only one person could use the brush at a time, making the job a little longer than was necessary. We left all the eggs on the table to dry out and for Grandpa to see when he came in.

When Grandpa Came in we showed him all the eggs and asked him if they were clean enough. He said that they looked real clean; clean enough for Grandma up at the store. We were real happy to hear him say that and started to dance around for joy. Then he said that we would have to get another brush from Mr. Gambuci when we went to on the next trip in and we would have to thank him for his idea, too.

Snake!

After supper Ronnie said, "Let's go over to the tomato patch and see how the tomatoes are doing." Away we went to the tomato patch on the other side of the creek and down at the foot of the Big Hill. The tomato patch wasn't right at the foot of the Big Hill. It was across a small field from the Big Hill next to the creek. But no matter, we went along the way and crossed the creek at the island then got to the tomato patch soon enough. We were just walking along the rows seeing if they needed hoeing.

Ronnie let out a shout that would wake the dead. "Snake!" he shouted. Sure enough a garter snake had made his home in the tomato patch. I picked up a hoe and started after the snake. I took one swing at it but the blade of the hoe came down just ahead of the darn snakes head. The snake stopped his forward motion and started to go back the way he came. That beat all, flat, clean and outright.

I took another pass at the snake and this time I missed him again. Well that left me wondering if I would always miss. I kept after him and kept swing the hoe every time I got a good chance at him. I kept missing him each time I swung the hoe at him. Just what was I supposed to do? I kept swinging the hoe and he kept dodging the blade on every swing. I was beginning to think that I was too small to swing the hoe right. I had been swinging the hoe pretty fast. Maybe I wasn't taking enough time in between swings.

So I decided to take my time as much as I could. But I didn't want him to get away from me. So I started to take a good aim each time I swung the hoe. This I did and on the first swing of the hoe I cut him clean in two leaving both halves writing around in his death throws. We then finished up with the tomato patch and were looking around for something else to do.

The evening was turning out to be one of those lazy, hazy eves of summer. We couldn't think of another thing to do. So, we went back to the island in the creek. We stripped down to our shorts and went for a swim. Boy! Was the water ever nice! It was just the right temperature. We stayed in the creek for the rest of the evening, coming out only when we heard Grandpa calling for us. It seems that Grandpa was in need of a few pieces of kindling and another batch of firewood for the kitchen stove. We got out of the water, dried ourselves as best we could and went out to the woodpile to get some wood for the stove and took it inside.

After that, we went to our sleeping places and got ourselves ready for bed, crawled under the covers of our bed on the mattress on the floor, and said that we wished that the house was settled down on its foundation. Enough of that wishing business, all we had to do was be ready to help as much as we could when the proper time came. With that we went to sleep, sleeping until the morning hours.

The next morning we got up earlier than usual and went out of the little house and down by the creek. We then walked along the creek until we were about down to the little garden that Grandpa had planted in the spring. I was looking in at the garden as we walked by it. Then suddenly I thought that I saw a movement among the plants. No, it couldn't be. Wait a minute. Let's look again. Sure enough there was something among the plants. "Let's go inside the garden fence to see what it is," I said. So up we went to the garden gate and opened the gate so we could go in. We went in and closed the gate after us. I led the way over to where I had seen the movement. When we got there we didn't see a thing.

We started to look around at the plants. We looked all around but we didn't see anything unusual. We got down on our knees to look under the plants real well. We looked and looked and didn't see a thing out of the ordinary. I said, "I must have been seeing things" and stood up. Just as I was standing up I happened to look across at the next plot of plants and there was another snake. A garden snake for sure, but a snake just the same. I quickly went over to the plants in that plot and looked again. There it was trying to hide and get away at the same time. I ran over to the gateway and got a shovel and came right back. Ronnie said that he had lost track of the snake so we got down on our hands and knees again to look under the plants. I finally spotted it near the end of a row of plants and shouted to Ronnie, "Here is where I saw the snake."

He said, "I can't see it at all, go and get the snake if you can." So I ran down to the area where I had seen the snake expecting to be able to see it again when I got there. Well I couldn't see it at all. I said to Ronnie, "I saw the snake slithering away by the end of the row right where I saw it the last time." Ronnie said, "I was standing over on the other side of the plot and I didn't see it at all." I said to him, "Get down on your knees and you will see it for sure." He did just that and he did see the snake, just as it was wiggling its way under another plant to hide once more, near the end of the plot.

That darned snake was about as quick as anybody in getting around and didn't waste a second getting to his next space. He could slither away and be gone in a flash and a slither he did. He was gone again and we didn't see where to this time. "Well," I said, "he's got to be here someplace, and that's for sure." So we went all around the patch and looked under each plant and we didn't see him any place. Then we got to thinking about the other patches close by. We started looking under all the plants in the close-by plots and we soon spotted him over in the next plot crawling up a plant trying to hide himself.

We went over to the next plot, bent down and we could see him wound around a plant up into its leaves. I reached into the plant and took hold of his snaky body. He didn't feel good at all to me and I couldn't decide whether to hold on to him or let go of him. I finally decided to let him go, and I did just that. He slithered away from me as fast as he could go into the next patch of plants.

I crouched down with my head on the ground to keep watching him and where he was going next. I said, "Ronnie get over to the other side of this plot and see if you can get a look at him too," and he did. Pretty soon he let out a holler, "Here he is right by the edge of the plot. I'll see if I can get him to come out of there and then we can get him for sure."

Ronnie went into the plot and shook the bush that the snake was trying to climb. Pretty soon down he came down and slithered his way over to the next plot and got under the plants again and was hiding for the umpteenth time. We were at a dead loss trying to think of a way to get him out in the open so we could kill him. Ronnie said, "I sure don't know what we can do to get him out in the open." I said, "Well I don't either but that isn't going to stop me. There's got to be a way of getting him out in the open without our knocking down all the plants in the garden. If we did knock even just some plants down we'd be in trouble with Grandpa for sure."

"So where do we go from here?" I said, looking so down and defeated. "Well I'll tell you where we can go from here. We can go over to the chicken coop and begin our chores for today." I said. With that we about gave up on the snake and we going to the gate to the garden area when suddenly, there ahead of us, slithering along the ground, was the snake. We were surprised to say the least to see it on the open ground. We took after it as fast as we could run out the gate and around the corner to the patch of grass just outside the garden area. When we got out there we couldn't see the snake any place.

Much as we tried to see the snake, we just couldn't spot it anywhere we looked. I said, "I'll go to the far end of the garden area and you stay here and watch, Ronnie." Away I went trotting down to the other end of the garden patch, watching all along the way for the snake. I got down to the other end of the garden area without seeing the snake again. I turned around to face Ronnie at the North end of the plot and wouldn't you know it, but there was the snake slithering away from the garden patch and getting out on the road that we had made.

What better opportunity could I have? I took the shovel, raised it over my head, and took a giant swing at the snake. I guess I must have missed it completely because there it was slithering away from me again. I kept on going after the snake and swinging the shovel at it time after time until he was into the grass on the far side of the road-way. Ronnie in the meantime had come up to where I was and was actively trying to keep the snake from going into the brush area along side the roadway.

This was a good move on his part because he kept the snake out in the open grass where we could see it and get another swipe at it with the shovel. I kept swinging the shovel at the snake hitting it a couple of times until at last I got a good shot at his head. Then kaboom the shovel came down with all the force of an avalanche and the snake lay dead in his slithering tracks.

Well, that was a good morning's chore done up properly, I might say without fear of contradiction. So we went over to the chicken coop to do daily chores. When we had gotten over to the coop we were tired from all the snake business from before. So we sat down for a little rest and the two of us could have gone to sleep right on the spot. Then we realized that it was still morning and got up to go back over to the little house.

Escape!

Morning started very early on the farm. Along about 5:00 am the rooster started his morning exercise, serenading one and all with his morning announcement of a new day. This new day was Tuesday, and it started off with a bang. We got out of our bed quickly and out the door for the chicken coop. When we got there, we found that some of the chickens had gotten out of the chicken coop and were roaming around the yard. "How the heck did they get out," we wondered. "Getting them all back into the coop was going to be a real job indeed!" Finally, after an hour or so we herded them all back into the chicken coop.

Then we had a minute to look around a little. Look we did and right there at the foot of the front wall was an opening. It wasn't a large opening, just enough room for a chicken to squeeze through. On closer inspection we found the birds themselves were to blame for this bit of shenanigans. They had pecked this little board loose from its moorings and had gotten out of the coop through the hole all on their own.

We decided that a likewise maneuver was needed on our part. Out the door and over to the sand pit we walked. Once there, we started looking around for a large stone big enough to block up the opening that the chickens had made for themselves. Then we found a stone that was just the right size, we took it back to the coop. We placed the stone into the hole that was made by the chickens. That little maneuver did the job nicely if I do say so myself.

After that we went out to the feed shed and got the morning repast for the birds. Then came the job of collecting the eggs. To gather all the eggs it took a half-hour or so filling our pockets and arms and making a couple of trips to the little house. When we had all the eggs over to the little house we started the cleaning detail. We pumped some water and started cleaning. We spent about four hours to get them clean and put in cartons. What a long job that was! We just had to get another brush to use and another one for a spare, too. Then we could be assured of getting the job done in at least half the time.

Once we had all the eggs cleaned up and put into cartons we were about done with today's chores. Grandpa had made us a good lunch and we had some free time on our hands. What should we do with all this free time? We asked each other. Well let's go see if the chickens are all right, so over to the chicken coop we went. When we got over there, there were about twenty chickens outside the coop. We didn't know why so many of the chickens were outside the coop.

We couldn't see any more holes in the front walls so the only thing we could do was to round them up and get them back inside the coop. So we began rounding them up. That was a hard job too. We'd be standing in one area waving our hands and making noises to get the chickens back into the coop. Only they didn't seem to want to go back into the coop, they were outside and they were going to stay outside. Try as we might we just couldn't get the chickens all back in their coop at the same time. We took a position on the two sides of the chickens and tried to herd them all together into the coop. That worked somewhat ok but it didn't get the whole bunch into the coop.

We had gotten all but four chickens into the coop and just couldn't seem to get their cooperation in the venture. We were tired ourselves and we sat down to rest a little. While sitting there resting I thought about eating, and just then the thought that the chickens might be hungry too gave me the idea that we should go get them some feed and use that to get them inside the coop. Up we got and over to the feed shed we went. We got a big scoop of feed out and shut the door. We took the scoop of feed over to the coop being careful to let the chickens see the scoop of feed. We went over to the coop and opened the door. Then we stepped inside the coop and with the chickens outside watching us, we spilled a little of the feed onto the floor. You should have seen the rush of the chickens still outside to get to the inside where we had spilled a little grain. That taught us something of a lesson about the chickens too. They got hungry just like we humans do.

The question remained though, how were the chickens getting out of the coop? We thought that we had put a stone in the last hole they were using and thought that that had put a stop to the chickens getting out. But they evidently had another hole or something that we didn't know about. I wondered where the hole was I said to myself and looked all over the coop walls to find it. But I didn't have any luck in finding a hole that was large enough to let a chicken through. As much as we looked at the walls we still couldn't see a hole that was large enough for a chicken to get through. About the only thing we could do was to get up early in the morning and come over to the coop to watch. Tomorrow would be as good a day as any. So we decided that tomorrow we would get up early and come over to watch the chickens as they came out of the building.

The next morning about 4 am we got out of bed, got dressed and went outside over to the chicken coop. When we arrived, there wasn't a chicken outside of the coop. That much was good news anyhow. It meant that the chickens were just not awake yet. But just wait a few more minutes to see. So we sat down and waited for the rooster to make his morning song debut. It was only about fifteen more minutes and the rooster was up and at them. With lots of volume he started in with his wake up call. Soon you could hear cackling racquet from all over the coop as the rest of the chickens woke up to the new day.

We waited with baited breath for the first of the chickens to come out through their hidden hole. We waited and waited and then waited some more, but not a chicken did come outside the coop. We were at a loss to figure out why the chickens had not come out. So we waited some more and soon it was getting to be breakfast time.

I said, "I'm hungry Ronnie, how about you?" "So am I!" he said. "Lets go get some breakfast." So over to the little house we went and when we got there we found Grandpa making us our breakfasts. He said, "Where have you been? I didn't even hear you when you went out." "Well Grandpa we were over to the chicken coop to see how the chickens were getting out," we replied. "Did you see how the chickens were getting out?" he asked. "No" we said. "They just weren't coming out while we were there. We'll have to go back after breakfast to see."

After breakfast it was clean up the dishes and put them away. We then went outside to go over to the chicken coop again. When we got to the coop there were several chickens outside. We just sat down and waited for some more to come out. Sure enough in about a half an hour more there was another chicken out side the coop. But we hadn't seen where he came from. Maybe it was around the back of the coop that the chickens were getting out without our seeing them in the act of getting out of the coop. So we went around to the back of the coop and there were another four or five chickens outside of the coop.

Again we were looking for the hole that the chickens were using, but trying our best to see the hole just wasn't good enough. So we sat down behind the coop and watched for the next chicken to come out. Soon there was another chicken just coming out thru the wall. We had the hole spotted and went right over to see it. It was another hole that we wouldn't think a chicken could get through. Now that we had it spotted we went over to the gravel pit to find a large enough rock to stop up the hole with.

We found a stone of about the right size and carried it back to the coop. When we got there we put the stone in the hole stopping all chickens from coming out that way again. Then we went around the front of the coop and started in getting all the chickens that were outside back together so we could get them all inside again. This was no small chore. We first had to round up all the chickens and then get them back inside. Well, rounding up the chickens wasn't so bad. We just had to use a little good judgment and pretty soon they were all corralled pretty good and Ronnie had the door open for them and in they went.

It seems like the chicken coop had some holes in it that would need our serious attention in the near future and we decided that the only thing we could do was to tell Grandpa about it. So we would have to go over across the creek again to find Grandpa and to tell him what we thought about the chicken coop. We went back across the creek again and found Grandpa working up at the new house. We said, "We had found out about the chicken coop hole," and he said, "I'm not surprised at all. I've seen the chickens outside of the coop before today from time to time."

He didn't seem too concerned until we told him about the varmint that we had seen. When we mentioned this to him he was genuinely interested and he told us to get the 22 with some shells and to be ready for him to go over to the chicken coop as soon as he got down to the little house. Down the hill we ran as fast as we could go and had the 22 and some shells waiting for Grandpa when he got back from the new house.

As soon as he got down from the new house we were out in the yard to meet him with the 22 and some shells. He said, "Lets get started," and away we went across the bridge to the chicken coop. Then he said, "Stay behind me now because I'm going to have to shoot if the varmint is here." As luck would have it, there was a varmint out in front of the chicken coop. Grandpa took a sighting at it and shot him deader than a door nail. So much for that varmint whatever he was.

Grandpa said, "Don't touch that varmint until you're sure its dead." So we didn't touch the varmint and started to tell him about the holes in the wall of the chicken coop. I said, "The first hole was in front of the coop right over here." I pointed to the place where we had put a stone to stop the chickens from coming out. Then I said, "The other hole is around the back of the coop." We went around to the back of the coop and I showed Grandpa where the hole was.

"Well it looks like we are going to have to do something about this problem pretty soon," he said. "I'll have to give it some thought to come up with an idea that you boys can work with. In the meantime, we still have all our chores to do so we'd better get at them." With that he turned back toward the little house and started to walk away.

Hunting Party

When we had our breakfasts Grandpa said "What are you boys going to do today?" I said, "We don't know of anything in particular." Ronnie said, "But we might go hunting." With that he said, "Well be careful and don't be late for our lunch." We got the 22rifle and started out the door. Ronnie said, "Let's go up to John Arco's place." We got up to the top of the long hill towards John Arco's place. We were walking along when we spotted two crows at the end of the hill. Ronnie took a shot at one of them and missed. We always missed the crows. I wonder what the good shooters would think.

Pretty soon we were in the woods near John Arcos' place. Walking along we heard something like kids playing but we couldn't see anyone else around. We stopped to listen for a while. We walked toward the sounds. Then we figured we'd better not get involved and started off to the West, back toward our farm. We crossed the fence that separated us from John Arco's farm, and I said, "Let's go see the woodchucks." Ronnie said, "What time is it?" It was about 10 o'clock by then, so we decided to go across the railroad bridge to save a little time.

Once across the bridge we headed down the tracks to the woodchuck mound that was up on a knoll alongside the tracks. We saw two woodchucks playing around outside of their holes. Ronnie, who was carrying the gun, stopped walking and took a shot. He hit the one closest to us and the other one made a dive for his hole. We ran up to the knoll and picked up the dead woodchuck. Were we ever proud! We'd show the old guys who were the best shots!

With that we picked up the dead woodchuck by his tail and started off for the farmhouse to show Grandpa the trophy. It was noon by the time we got to the farmhouse. Grandpa was in the process of making lunch. We got cleaned up and came into the cooking area looking for a place to sit down. Grandpa said, "You boys sit on your sleeping blankets." We did, and were ready for our lunch. He said, "You boys have done well with the woodchuck. Leave it where I can get to it. I'll cook it up for supper today." Together Ronnie and I made some awful sounds that expressed our loathing of the idea. That seemed to end the idea and Grandpa didn't say another word. He just fed us our lunch in silence. We got to thinking if we had hurt him in anyway, and said so to him. He just shrugged and said, "No."

After lunch we again went out hunting again. This time though we took the farm dog Spike with us for a little friendly companionship. Spike was a fun loving animal to say the least. He was always running around and barking up a storm. He was just fun to have along with us. Today we went to the west side of the farm, up to the potato hill to look for some woodchucks. We got Spike to be quiet so as not to scare any woodchucks that might be there into going back into their holes.

When we got to the top of the hill, about fifteen minutes later, there were five woodchucks digging away for all they were worth. They were after Grandpa's potatoes. We had to stop them! Ronnie had the 22 and he took fast aim and shot one of the woodchucks. Man! That made two woodchucks in one day! Some kind of record, I'd say. Ronnie gave the rifle to me and said for me to shoot one too. All the woodchucks had long since jumped into their holes, and there weren't any more for me to shoot. With that turn of events we decided to go back to the mound of woodchucks by the railroad tracks.

Down the hill we went and across the field. I said, "Lets go over to the sand and gravel pit behind the chicken coop." Off we went to the gravel pit across the creek but first we had to go down by the little house to get some more shells for the 22. We stopped long enough at the little house to pick up some more shells and then we were off to the big sand pit behind the chicken coop. When we got across the bridge over the creek we saw a varmint of some kind right in front of the chicken coop. It disappeared before we could get a shot at it, so we just kept going over to the coop. If we saw it again we were going to take a shot at it for sure.

We opened the door to the coop and found to our amazement that all of the chickens were up on the rafters and there was the varmint on the floor of the coop. When it saw us come in, it made a quick trip to the coops wall and disappeared before we could get a shot off at it. We said, "Darn it anyhow!" We went over to the wall where the varmint had disappeared and looked for the hole. Sure enough we found a small hole in the wall that was just large enough for the varmint to get in through. We said, "Lets go find a rock big enough to stop up the hole"

So we went over to the gravel pit behind the chicken coop to look of a rock that was about the right size. We soon found one and started back for the coop. When got there we went inside and found the hole again. Then we put the rock into the hole and it was just the right size to stop up the hole. "Nothing will be able to get in though there any more," we said.

Then as a change of pace we decided to go up to the woodchucks mound by the railroad track. So off we went back across the creek and up to the top of the grain shed hill. When we got up there we stopped and looked over at the woodchucks mound on the other hill. It must have been around two hundred yards from where we were over to the woodchucks mound by the railroad tracks. Quite a ways that's for sure. While we were looking over there we saw a chuck outside of his den hole and got toward wondering if we could hit it from where were.

It was my turn to shoot the 22 and I stopped and sighted it on the chuck. I didn't know if I could hit it or not, but it was worth a try. I sighted on the chuck and the gun was waving around quite a bit. What I needed was a solid aiming place. I stopped aiming and began to look around for something to support me while I aimed the gun. I didn't see a thing so I just sat down with my knees up for support. Then sitting down I raised the 22 up to sight it on the chuck way over on top of his mound. This time with my elbows on my knees, my sighting the 22 was much more steadier and I could get a good aim at the chuck. I finally took a shot when I had the chuck in my sights, and the chuck was nowhere to be seen. He had disappeared completely. So I figured that I had missed him.

Ronnie and I started to walk down the hill we were on and across the pasture fence and started up the hill where the chuck's den was. We finally made it up there and began to look around. We found the dead chuck in the den hole and pulled it out of the den. That was a pretty darn good shot if I do say so myself. It must have been about two hundred yards from the other hilltop to this one. Pretty good shooting I said to myself, pretty darn good shooting. I'd have to tell Grandpa about this that's for sure.

Ronnie and I were all fired up about shooting the chucks and said, "Let's go over to potato hill to see if there are any more out and about." Ronnie said. So we just left the dead chuck in the hole of the den as a warning to the other chucks and went on out way. It was quite a ways over to potato hill from where we were so it took us about a half hour to get over there. We finally made it to potato field and looked around the patch to see if there were any chucks about.

We saw that there were about four or five chucks out in the field just going at getting the potatoes from the ground for all the were worth. It was Ronnies turn to shoot the 22, and he said very quietly,

"Let's get over by the den holes before I shoot." Well we did do just that and were in a position to shoot when the chucks looked up and saw us between them and their den holes. They stopped in their tracks and Ronnie was ready for them. He shot one of them deader than dead.

Then he gave the 22 to me and I shot one too. That makes three chucks that we got today. Some kind of record for sure, and we did it all with a little single shot 22rifle. Some kind of pretty good doings I'd say! That's for sure! That's for darned sure! What were we going to do with all these chucks anyhow? We decided to just leave them by the holes as a reminder to the rest of them what they had coming to them the next time we caught them out in the field. So we picked up the two dead chocks and put one over by each of the den holes that the chucks had come out of.

We decided that we had had enough hunting for one day and started back for the farm buildings, and were just passing the Haunted Woods. We said, "Let's go through the woods area to day." So we entered the haunted woods and were enjoying the cool air. The haunted woods were just about three acres of woods at the bottom of the last hill that the new house had climbed. It was cool inside them and well shaded by tree limbs that were all coved with algae forming a roof over our heads. We enjoyed our walk through the woods and came out the other side just below the last hill that the new house had climbed.

It was up this last hill that we were climbing when Spike, the dog, took off for parts unknown. He just ran for all was worth up the hill and out of sight. The Good Lord only knew were he was headed, because we didn't have a clue to where he was going. Well we said, "We will find out when we get up to the top of the hill." Sure enough, when we got up to the top of the hill there was Spike, just lying down and waiting for us to get up to him.

My New Friend, the Deer

We had been up to the top of potato hill where had shot a woodchuck and were on our way back to the barn area when we decided to go through the haunted woods. We entered the woods from the near side and it was all covered with algae and the like. The trees were all shaggy with vine and leaf hanging down and it was cool inside despite it being seventy or more outside the woods. We all three went into the woods, Ronnie, Spike, and I, and almost immediately Spike went into his pointing mode with one front leg raised with an intent stare to our left. We froze and didn't move a muscle just waiting for something to make a run for the outside of the wood.

Just then a small deer jumped up and started running toward the fields. We were so surprised that we just stood there and watched. When the deer got almost to the edge of the woods it stopped, turned around and looked at us. We were so shocked that we just stood there and tried to keep from saying anything because we were afraid that we would scare the deer. Spike was the anxious one. He kept tugging at his collar trying to get away from us and go after the deer. We had a heck of a time restraining him. We finally got him settled down.

The deer was still standing there watching us. He just stood there and watched everything we did. Ronnie turned around and started to go back out of the woods. He went as carefully and as quietly as he could. The deer just stood there and watched us. It was ready to bolt at a moments notice. Ronnie left Spike and I just standing there. He went slowly and very quietly picking his steps carefully. The deer in the meantime just stood its ground and watched us with a clear eye.

Pretty soon Ronnie came back in the woods with his pockets and hands full of grass that he had picked. He extended his handful of grass to the deer. The two of us began to talk very quietly to the deer and the deer just stood there and watched us. If there was ever a time to be frustrated, this was it for sure! We then started to very slowly, easily, creep up on the deer. The darned deer just stood there like a dumb ox. It just kept his head turned our way, watching us and where we were going. It took us about thirty minutes or so to get up to where the deer was standing.

We were still holding out our hands with the nice green grass toward the deer. All of a sudden the deer came over to us and started nibbling on the grass. Were we ever surprised! Man alive! You could have used our heads for Billy Clubs! We were so surprised! The deer just kept on nibbling and even let us pet her while she was eating. For the first time in our lives we became true nature lovers! I left Ronnie there to feed the deer some more and I went out of the woods very quietly and picked another bunch of grass. Spike in the meantime had cooled off some and stopped trying to get away from us. I think he sensed that this was an important situation. The deer was very calmly eating the grass that we had provided and let us pet her all the while.

The deer kept nuzzling our hand each time we'd put it down just as if she liked it. We got to wondering what to do with her and said lots of things. Until I said, "Let's take her up to the old birdcage behind the new house." I no more than had the words out of my mouth when Ronnie piped in with, "Yeah. But will she come?" "All we can do is try." I said. With that we took the rope that we had saved for Spike and tied it around her neck. We tied a square knot, not a slipknot so the deer wouldn't get scared. Next we both went out and got a lot of grass. A LOT of grass, and filled both our pockets and our hands, and then came back for the deer. She was just standing there waiting for us. We said, "Let's go."

That led to all sorts of shenanigans. We took up the rope and started to walk, but the deer wouldn't have anything to do with that. She just lay down with her front legs folded beneath her, looking at us so forlornly that we knew that something wasn't right. We tried to explain that we were only going to take her up to the old birdcage by the new house. This went on and on until we sat down with her and petted her very gently. We tried to explain that it was in her best interests to come along. Finally, we quit feeding grass to her and I thought that she might have caught on to some of our antics.

This time when we started out she came right along with us. Not only out in the open, but also up the little hill that was the last hill that the house had negotiated. We were getting close to the cage and moving along quite nicely. Then Ronnie went on ahead to get the door to the cage opened that left me together with a fairly cooperative deer. I stopped to gather her up in my arms. She came along nicely and was apparently happy to be carried. I took off for the cage and was soon there. It was only a few feet away from me. Then Ronnie closed the gate when I got there and I put the deer down, to get to know her new surroundings a little. She came right back to me and nuzzled me to take her out of the cage. I said for Ronnie to go get a scoop of bran for her, which he did right off

When he came back with the scoop full of bran he only dumped it on the ground of the cage, just inside the gateway. But that was good enough for the deer. She started in eating the bran right away like she had had bran every day of her young life. Ronnie in the meantime had gone off to get her some water to drink. Boy did she ever drink! She drank like it was going out of style.

At least the deer was getting used to the cage area. We stayed and played with her until we heard Grandpa calling for us to come in. So, we went down to the little house. The first thing we had to do was get cleaned up for supper and then sit down to eat. We didn't know what to tell Grandpa about the deer so we didn't say a word, right then anyway. We decided to wait for a more favorable time to break the news to Grandpa, which would be tonight, of course. Tomorrow he would be going out by the new house up on the hill and he would see the deer up there and begin wondering where she had come from.

After supper we tried to tell him about the deer, but some how we just couldn't do it. We decided to wait for the morning chores to get done, before we said anything at all. The next morning we got up early, went out and cut some green grass and took it up to the deer. We had to get her some water too, so we went down to the creek and got a whole pail full. We took that up to her and played with her for a while until we heard Grandpa coming up the hill. He was looking at the house and the foundation walls and didn't notice us at first.

Then he wanted to know what we were doing. We were standing in front of the cage, kind of blocking his view so he didn't see the deer right off. I said, "Grandpa, you had better come over here." He got a real questioning look on his face and he walked over to where we were standing. Not until he got close to the cage did he see anything out of the ordinary. Then he jumped back and said, "There is a deer behind you! Wait and I'll go get the rifle!" We started in to tell him it was our tame deer that we had brought in yesterday afternoon.

We could tell right off that he didn't believe us for a minute. So, we went into the cage and took her a handful of bran. She came right over to us without hesitating a bit and started to eat from our hands. Grandpa was just amazed. He couldn't believe what his old eyes were seeing. He looked once, and then he looked again. Darned if that wasn't a new deer this spring. The boys had gotten it to get in the cage without so much as a bleat out of it.

All of a sudden he had so many questions. How did you get it up here, was the main one, I guess. We began to tell him about yesterday. We told him about Ronnie shooting the woodchuck and we told him about Spike spotting the deer. Then we told him about feeding it some grass, and how we had taken the deer out of the woods and started up the small hill with it. We told him how I had carried the deer to the cage and how Ronnie had run down and got some bran for it to eat.

We told him how the deer had seemed to like it when we came up to the top of the little hill and placed her in the cage; how she had liked the bran that Ronnie had brought her. Grandpa had this incredulous look on his face during all this time that we could tell that he didn't believe a word we said. Still and all, there was the proof of what we said, standing on its own four legs in the cage, eating from our hands. Grandpa said, "That beats everything I've ever heard of or seen! And you didn't shoot it either," he said rather incredulously.

Now all that remained was how were we going to keep her there with winter coming and all. That particular thought had not occurred to us at all. Just what were we going to do? We couldn't just leave her there without provisions of any kind. We had to start school in the next month and wouldn't be around at all during the weekdays to look after her and feed her at all. Well now we could just leave her be by itself, or we could pay attention to her and play with her everyday as long as she staid there. We decided that the later was the best way to handle the situation and went on playing with her.

These were some pretty important questions that needed to be answered before the week was out, that's for sure! Grandpa was still unbelieving. He said that we had to cut green grass for her to eat, and had to keep her in bran as well. Then he suggested that we go down to the barn and get a couple of forks full of hay and bring them up here for the deer to sleep on. This seemed like a good idea. Off we went to the barn to get the hay. In no time we were back up at the cage carrying enough hay for seven or eight deer to sleep on. When the deer saw us coming, it just watched us open the cage and put the hay down in a corner for her to sleep on.

The first thing it did was to try to eat some of the hay. Of course, we didn't intend for the deer to eat the hay! Ronnie and I went over to the hay and we laid down on it hoping the deer would get the idea and lay down herself. After eating some more of the green grass we had cut for her, the deer came over to the hay where we were and began nosing around the two of us. It was about time for her to take a nap and we said so to her. She must have understood us because she lay down herself and in a few minutes was soon asleep.

We were so proud to have found a pet deer that was so darned smart! You could have struck up the band! We got up quietly and went out of the cage quietly closing the gate, so as not to waken the deer. The rest of the morning we spent down at the creek looking for shiny stones but we didn't find any. When Grandpa called us for dinner, we were ready to eat. We got cleaned up and went in for our lunch. We set the table with silverware and plates and got ready to eat lunch.

After lunch we said that we had better go see how the deer was coming along. We did this, picking up some more green grass on the way. We weren't at all surprised to find her lying down but took her some of the fresh grass that we had cut for her. She stood up but was very wobbly on her feet and she didn't look at all good. I went over to her and took her up in my arms. She seemed to like that and turned her head up to me. Then without any further ado she turned her head toward me and licked my face, just as if she was saying thank you. I couldn't believe it. I just couldn't believe it! Then as if to say, "Thank you so very much," she licked my face again.

I asked Ronnie to go get Grandpa, and he did, running all the way down to the barn. I don't know what he told Grandpa but the two of them were hurrying up the hill as fast as they could go. When they got up to the cage they were huffing and puffing like all get out. The first thing was to stop long enough to catch their breaths. Then Grandpa wanted to know what the trouble was. I told him that I didn't think the deer was at all well. Grandpa wanted to see why I thought that way, so I put the deer down on its feet. Almost right away the deer's back legs folded up and down she sat. Grandpa took one look and said that he thought she was sick and we should have a vet look at her right away.

Ronnie took that as a death sentence and started to cry, I did too, I guess. That little deer had come to mean so much to me and to Ronnie too. Grandpa said to let him have a few minutes and then he would get the car and we would take the little deer in to town for the Vet to look at it. We said sure and then sat down to wait a few minutes for Grandpa. In just a few minutes Grandpa came driving up the hill with the car. He parked as close as he could and we got in the car with the deer in my arms, away we went into town.

You never saw such a group of people, with Grandpa leading the way, me carrying the deer, and Ronnie bringing up the rear trouping into the Vet's office. Once there we were ushered into the vet's inner office without any fan fare what so ever. The Vet wanted to take a look at the deer as quickly as he could. He told me to set the deer down and to allow it to stand alone for a while. This I did immediately and the deer stood there on wobbly legs for a while and then she collapsed on the floor again. The vet wanted to know what we had been feeding her. We said that we had given her much green grass and some bran.

The vet said that alone should not make her sick and that he wanted to keep her for a few days. Grandpa said he could if she got a nice cage to stay in. The vet said she'd have the very best and took her up in his arms. She didn't like that a bit! She struggled to free herself of that grasp and came over to me. She won my heart forever with that move! I said to the vet, "Which cage do you want her in?" and he showed me the one that I should put her in. I picked up the deer and took her over to the cage and gently put her inside.

The deer just lay there and I reached over and petted her gently behind her ears. It was very apparent that she did not want to stay there at all. So, I said to Grandpa and Ronnie to go and I'd stay with her until I could get her calmed down enough to stay by herself.

Grandpa and Ronnie left and I stayed by the cage and I tried to calm her down a little. I called the vet over to try to introduce him to the deer. I asked him to wash his hands first which he did.

He then came over and let the deer smell his hands. This went over very good with the deer. Then he began to pet her behind the ears. She seemed to like that, so he sat there and scratched her neck a little. That seemed to be all she required to get to know the vet. By this time it was getting to be close to five o'clock and I was getting hungry. I had to go from east end of Mahoning Street way down to the west end of Lincoln Street to get to the store and get some lunch. That had to be close to a mile at least, so I figured I'd better get started.

Going along the Mahoning Street hill I met up with some of my friends and they all wanted to know where I was going and where I had been. I said, "I'm going to the store and I had been at the vets". Then they wanted to know why had I gone to the vets place. I couldn't tell them the truth, so I lied a little and said that Grandpa had left me there when he came to town on a fast trip, and let me walk to the store from there. They all bought that story pretty quickly and that was the end of that. Lord only knows what would have happened if any of them found out about the deer. I certainly wasn't going to tell them that we had brought a sick deer in to the vets place.

I didn't like telling a lie about it. As quickly I could, I broke away from them all, and started to go to the store again. In a little while I got there and all I had to do was explain myself to the women. With many cautions to keep as quiet as they could be about what I was going to tell them. They all agreed that they would not say a word to anyone. With that agreement, I began to tell them about the deer, about our finding the deer in the woods, about our taking the deer up to the cage and leaving her overnight.

Then I told about how we had found her early this morning. I told about our driving up to town after the chores were done and had taken her to the veterinarians place up on Mahoning Street. With all that, there seemed to be some incredulous looks on the faces of the girls. I had said it didn't matter if they believed me not, as long as they wouldn't tell about it at all. They all agreed to be quiet and would not say a word to anyone.

That little truce that we had made lasted until the next morning. I had come down stairs and was hunkered down behind a couple of cases of oranges when I heard Auntie Ada starting to tell one of the customers about the deer. She was telling it like there was no tomorrow. Going at it like it was the last day on earth. I stood up at about then and said rather loudly, "Ada!" She stopped talking, and then she said for me to be quiet. That, in my humble opinion, took a lot of nerve! A real lot of nerve! It was too late now. The cat was out of the bag for sure, now.

That left me hanging out to dry. Why couldn't at least one woman keep a promise not to say anything? If she had to talk about something, why not talk about the nice weather we were having or almost anything else. It left me with a bad taste in my mouth. Now the word would get all over town for sure. All my friends would hear about it and they would know that I had a deer up at the vets place.

What would I tell Grandpa and Ronnie? As soon as the customer had left, I went out and hightailed it for the vets place. When I got there the vet didn't want me to come inside. I couldn't think of a good reason not to go in, so I just barged into the back room where the deer was in a cage. At least the deer was glad to see me. When I went over to her cage, she tried to stand up but couldn't. She looked so forlorn and helpless. Then I spotted a switch on the floor by the cage and started to put two and two together. If this was the kind of treatment that could be expected from a vet, the vet had no business treating any sick animal. Darn his hide anyway! I undid the cage door and took the deer out.

Then carrying the deer I went out the vets' door. The vet wanted to know where I thought I was going. I told him that I was going to my Grandmas store and that I would tell everyone about his beating my deer. With that, I left, and started to make my way for the store. Pretty quick all the kids long the route were catching up with me and they all wanted to see the deer. At the corner of Third Ave and Railroad Street where there was a vacant lot, I stopped and sat down. I held the deer in my arms.

All the kids wanted to come and see the deer so I told them that she was sick and not to expect her to be jumping about. This satisfied almost every one of them. There were a few that weren't convinced so I told them to stay back of the crowd. The others I let come up one or two at time to see the deer. They all had a chance to come and see the deer. They were oowing and awing away like crazy. Then finally the doubters said they wanted to look too, so I said they could, providing they behaved themselves and kept the noise down. They said, "All right."

Then, in a dejected sort of mood, they came forward to see the deer. When they got up to the spot to see the deer, they were amazed to say the least and started to shout and holler as loud as could be. Right away I told them to stop the hollering or I was going home and none of them would get a chance to see the deer. They kept the noise down to a pounding roar at least. I stayed there for about an hour when I said that I had to go home. They all came, including the doubters in the crowd, came along with me.

Soon I was back at the store but I had nowhere to put the deer. I got a few of the older boys to put together a cage of some sort using the fence poles that were just laying around in the shed. They did a pretty good job nailing the poles about two inches apart to a sturdy floorboard and then said, "OK. It's ready." With that I took the deer over to its new cage and set her in it. She must have been pretty worn out by then and just laid down to sleep some. I guess she had it coming after all I had put her through that day. Ronnie and Grandpa came into town at about four that afternoon and said that they had to get right back to do the afternoon chores.

I told Grandpa what I had found at the vet's place. He said that I wasn't too upset about it and that he would take care of the vet when he came to town on Saturday. Then I asked if there was another vet in town. He said no there wasn't, but maybe there was one over in Virginia that we could use. With that he said, "Let's go boys." We got the deer out of the cage, got in the car and started off for the farm once more. We took the Dupont Road so as to miss the bridgework that the county was doing at Mohka's place. Soon we were at the farm once again. Grandpa went to see about getting his chores done. We took the little deer up to her cage and gently set her down on the matting of hay that Ronnie and I had brought there. Then we had to get our chores done also.

Off we went to the chicken coop. It seemed as though the chickens hadn't missed us as much as we thought they should. All of them seemed uninterested in us until we started passing out the grain, then they all perked right up with their cackling and strutting stuff. We gathered up all the eggs, at least as many as we could carry in one trip. We took the first load over to the little house and then came back for the next load. We took that over to the house and came back a third time for another load of eggs.

Boy, this was turning into a fine egg day. We took this last load back to the house and got ready to clean them up. We counted five dozen eggs and we started cleaning them up. Grandpa came in and sat down to help us with the cleaning. He made the job go faster than ever. Pretty soon we were putting the last of them into the egg cartons, and Grandpa said it's time for supper now. We got cleaned up and ready to eat and set the table with silverware and plates in no time at all.

Grandpa did a wonderful job getting supper on the table. We had noodles with homemade sauce, meat slices, and beans. Grandma had fixed this supper for us the other day when she was down here at the farm. I always said that the food we got here was better than the food we got anywhere else, bar none. I guess I was exaggerating little, to say the least. Anyway it was a good supper, and we ate our fill. After supper we went up to the cage to see the deer and found her sound asleep. With that, we said we had better get to bed also. We ran back to the house and got ourselves ready for bed. That took us about five minutes and we jumped into our sleeping mats and were asleep in no time at all.

The next day we were up early getting our breakfast early and then went to the cage to see the deer. We found her wide awake but lying down again. When she saw us she let out a little noise. We gave her the water we were carrying up for her, she drank from it a long time and then she stood up and came over to me. She put her nose on my leg and gave it a little shove, as if to say thank you. I bent over and hugged her with the tears just running out of my eyes. It was so good to see her up and around a little bit.

Then Grandpa came up the hill and said that we should go to Virginia to see the vet over there. He also said that we should put a rope around her neck. I hated to do that, but he said to, so I did it. I then led the deer out of the cage and down to the car. Grandpa got in, as did Ronnie, and we were off on the little trip to Virginia.

Man, was this an adventure for all of us! We took the back roads over to the fine little town of Virginia, just so the Deer could get a glimpse of some different countryside. Sure enough she was looking at everything along the route. She didn't seem to miss a thing going by. Pretty soon we got to Virginia and Grandpa said we had to get a phone book. We spotted a telephone sign on a building and stopped there so he could go in to call the vets. Grandpa went into the building. He was gone a long time, we were wondering why. About an hour later he came back to the car. He came over to the car and leaned in the window and said to us, "You two crooks are going right home." With that he got in the car and said that the vet had told him it was illegal to have a deer.

What the heck was that? What did he mean by that? Grandpa said that the State of Minnesota said that it was not legal to keep a deer by anyone not a public zoo. We'd show them a thing or two! Then Grandpa said that we could take the deer right in to the vet's office so that he could try to tell what was wrong with her. I said, "Let's do it Grandpa." With that, he started off to find the vet's place.

We had to go out to the near North side of town to get to the vet's place. We were looking all over the street for the vet's place and couldn't see one at all. After driving up and down the street several times a man came out of one house and stood in the middle of the road. He stopped us on our next pass and then he said, "Are you looking for the vet's place?" "Yes," we said, "We are."

"OK then, follow me," he said, and follow him we did. We found ourselves in the alley behind the houses. Then we saw a small sign that said Veterinarian. Grandpa got out of the car and went into the vet's office. He no more than got in there than he was out again with a man following him. He came over to the car and said, "Let me have a look at the little thing." We opened our door and said, "Please come around to our side." He did and when he got close to the deer, the deer got all excited and tried to get out of my hands. Then I told him the story of the day at the vet's office in Hibbing. The poor little thing was scared out of her wits when she got a smell of the vet coming near.

Thinking that this vet might be as bad as the first one, I said to Grandpa, "Let's go!" Grandpa explained to the vet why I was concerned and told him about our visit to the vet in Hibbing and how the vet there had beaten her with a branch of a tree. The vet just stood there with a look of disbelief on his face. Grandpa said, "If you don't believe it call the vet in Hibbing and ask him."

The vet looked over the deer and tried to assess why the deer was acting the way it was, but couldn't find anything wrong. He would have to do more extensive testing. Grandpa then paid the guy two dollars for his time and got back in the car, which was more than I would have given him, that's for sure.

We drove a long way going back to the farm before anybody said anything. Then, as if someone had turned on a switch, we all started talking at once. First I wanted to know who that vet was anyhow. Grandpa said that I should not talk so loudly. Then he said, "We got the deer, so lets go back to the farm and take care of her." Without further discussion on the subject, we continued on our way back to the farm.

The deer seemed to be sleeping in my arms and hardly moved a bit on our way. It also seemed genuinely surprised when we got out of the car up by her cage. I carried her over there to the cage and set her down on the bed of hay that she was used to. Then we went out to the field and cut some more green grass for her and Grandpas said, "Don't forget about her water." Ronnie went to get some water while I just sat down with her and petted her. Ronnie came back with the water in a pail that was full to the brim. He set it down and the deer seemed to know that it was for her. She stood up on her four legs and wobbled a little bit. Then over she went to the pail of water and drank her fill. After that she went over to Ronnie to be petted.

She seemed to be getting stronger as the day wore on. She even went over to eat a little bran. Ronnie and I stayed with her there in the cage for the rest of the day. When we got up to go eat she sort of whimpered a little, and we didn't know what to do. We just left her there in the unclosed cage and started down to the little house to eat. She just stayed in the cage until we had gotten about half way down to the house.

Again she let out a little bleep of sound and came running down the hill to us. She had the little rope in her teeth and laid it down in front of us, looked up and bleeped again. We couldn't do anything but cry and bent down to hug her tightly. She seemed to know that that maneuver was of pure unadulterated love of boys for an animal. She let out a little bleep of sound licked my face. Boy! If that wasn't something to see and have! I'll tell you it was the greatest thing that ever happened to us on the farm! Bar none!

She was there in the house with us to stay I guess, so I went out to get her some more green grass and little bit of bran and came right back so as not to miss a thing. Ronnie was playing with her when I got back with the grass and bran. She came right over to me and rubbed against my leg, then went to eat some of the grass. Ronnie went down to the creek for a pail of water for her and she seemed to know it, because she went to the door and just stood there until Ronnie came back with the water. Then she drank her fill and came over by me to lie down.

Grandpa was watching all this, of course, and said that he had never ever seen nor heard of such a display by an animal. He was just flabbergasted and went on, cooking our dinner. So I set the table with the silverware and the dishes. When dinner was ready we went to the table and sat down to eat.

The deer came over with us and seemed to want to sit at the table too. She finally got the idea that she wasn't invited to be at the table with us, and went over by the open door and lay down again. She was a member of the family now for sure. After our lunch we decided that we should go hunting again so we got the 22 and went out to see if Spike was in a mood to go with us. Sure enough, he was ready to go. We didn't know what he would do when he spotted the deer, so I picked up the little deer and then let Spike smell her to get to know her a little.

Neither one of them liked the idea in the least. The deer squirmed around in my arms to get away from the dog. Spike, as well, let out a bark and was jumping up on me to get at the deer. We kept telling him, "No, Spike!" until he finally began to understand that the deer was a friend and wasn't to be molested. With a lot of petting and quiet talk the deer began to settle down some too. With that, Ronnie and I settled down a little too and then we started off on our hunting trip. We went up to her cage and got the little rope to tie around her neck. She didn't mind a bit when I tied the rope kind of loosely and walked calmly along with us. Spike was a little annoyed that we had a new friend, but only at first.

Spike had gotten the word for sure by then. He was behaving quite nicely as we walked through the fields. We were heading up toward John Arcos place and enjoying the outing, when we came to the line fence and the little deer became a little violent. It was obvious that she didn't want to go beyond the fence, so we decided not to go either. What kind of turn of events was this anyhow? Why would the deer be afraid of the line fence, we asked ourselves. There has to be a reason we thought. What could it be? The answer wasn't apparent, at least not to us.

Done with hunting and bagging nothing, it was time to go home. We meandered down to the chicken coop by way of the sand pit. When we got there we remembered that we had not done our chores yet. We started in by getting the fresh hay for the nests and picked up most of the eggs. Then we went to take the eggs over to the house. We decided to leave the deer there at the chicken coop since we were coming right back anyway. We had our pockets and arms as full as we could make them and ran all the way over to the house with all the eggs. Then we came right back and there was Spike chasing the chickens off the poor deer. It seems the chickens had taken a liking to the deer and were just trying to make their likes known by loudly cackling and jumping up on the deer. Spike didn't seem to like that idea a bit and was doing his best to teach the chickens that wasn't allowed. He'd snap at them when they got too close to the deer and would bark kind of loudly. Of course, loudly was all he knew how to bark, that, and a low growl.

Don't get me wrong; Spike was some kind of good farm dog, to say the least. He was a good watchdog, the very best. He could even keep the outsiders from coming onto the farm from across the fields. Grandpa and Spike would go up the pasture hill to get the cows and move them to the barn. Then Spike would sit with them until grandpa came up to put them in their stations. He was always good to the cattle and would just lay down on his stomach with his head up and feet out in front of him, ever on the alert. He would just let the cows do whatever they wished except to cross the stream. I think that's why he was so good around the deer. He knew enough to be watchful and to not interfere when the other animals were where they should be.

That is why we could leave the deer at the open gate to the cage and never have to worry about the deer getting out. Of course the two of them were getting along famously well. We had come to this conclusion quite often in the week that the deer was there. We could take her up to the cage to leave her with the cage gate open while we went somewhere. The two of them got along just great—so much so, that we never had to worry a bit about her at all when Spike was there. Spike would always take up his duties as watchdog-caretaker whenever the need arose. He performed with outstanding skill each time it was required of him.

We left some grass and bran for the deer and went off hunting again, to see the woodchuck den on top of the knoll by the railroad tracks. There were two woodchucks out of the den and when we got close enough, one ran for its hole. After taking careful aim, I shot the other. That was OK by us. There was always another day starting tomorrow morning when the rooster crowed. It was Ronnie's turn to carry the gun again and he took it. The two of us started out for the hill top potato field to see if the 'chucks were out.

We thought that we should be awful quiet going up there and we got down on our hands and knees as we started up the hill. We went up the hill as quiet as we could and didn't make a sound. When we got up there we found that we were about at the far part of the potato patch near where the chucks had their holes. We looked out at the potato patch and could see three big chucks all facing the other way, so we got into position between them and their holes.

We had already loaded the 22 so we were ready to shoot. I heard a dog bark off in the distance a ways and the chucks heard it too. They all three started for their holes immediately and then they all saw us standing there and put on the brakes and stopped their run. We got one of them in our sights and fired the 22. Boom, and one of the chucks was dead! I went as fast as I could reloading the 22 and gave it to Ronnie to shoot at another, which he did quickly. There was another chuck dead. Two in less than a minute! Boy wouldn't Grandpa be proud of us for that! For sure! Three dead chucks in a day! That kind of day was good in my book any day!

That about made our day and we started off for the house after we went out and got the two dead chucks and stuffed their dead bodies into two of their holes. That should make them think twice before coming back again. With that we started to go back to the house. When we were going up the hill just past the haunted woods the little deer came running out to meet us. She ran right up to us, got behind us, and then she started walking with us toward her cage. When we got there Spike was nowhere to be seen. We thought that that was awful strange. When we had put the deer back in her cage, we had little time to look around for Spike. There was another car in the yard that hadn't been there when we went out. It must have been Spike that we heard barking before.

We went down to the house to see who was visiting us. To our surprise here was my Mother and Father. What the heck were they doing here at the farm on a weekday anyhow? Guess it must have been pretty important to bring them out here on a weekday. We went in the house and said hello. My mother said right out that they came down to the farm to get Ronnie, because he was going to have to go to Tucson with his mom and my sister Pat. Mom said that Pat had been sick with pneumonia and needed to get some dry air for her lungs to get healed up right.

That put a crimp in anything that we might have planned for sure. They had made reservations for the three of them on the train for tomorrow night leaving from Duluth, and my Dad was driving them to Duluth to catch the train. There was nothing we could say or do. We just went about getting our stuff ready and pretty soon we were ready. I told my Dad about the deer and said I was worried about it. My Grandpa said that he would look after the deer right away that day. That was OK with me and soon we were off for town, after I said goodbye to the deer. Then I did go up to the cage and took her in my arms to say goodbye to her, then down the hill again and we got in Dad's car and started off for town.

All of this was so sudden that it didn't even have a chance to sink in yet. While we were driving my Mother said that the apartment above the popshop was almost done and we could go see it on Monday of next week. I asked how long Pat and Ronnie were going to be gone. They said that they didn't know for sure but they thought about a year or so, maybe longer. That didn't set too well with me. I thought that they would be gone for a week or maybe even two weeks. I didn't think that much time would be required to clear up a little cold. Both Ronnie and I were pretty quiet for the rest of the ride into town. When we got to town Ronnie said that he would miss me very much and I said the same to him. We were both kind of crying a little bit.

In the morning we got up early and helped Ronnie get packed up for the trip that night. Patsy and Ronnie's mom also had plenty of packing to do. Seems like we were running back and forth, up and down all the day long, but it was only until about noon and then my dad said, "Let's go!" Soon, my Mom, Dad, Pat, Auntie Mary and Ronnie were gone in the car for Duluth. Seems like we didn't even have time for a goodbye before they were all gone from sight. Mom and Dad would be home late this evening I hoped. The rest of the day was real lonesome to say the least.

Two Important People

With Ronnie gone, this was going to be pretty lonely for sure. With Patsy gone too, it would make it twice as lonely. Of all the people that could be gone, those two were the most important ones for sure. Without them I would be surely lost. Ronnie was always with me at the farm and Patsy was always at home for me. Patsy was good to me. She took me up to the library with her whenever she went and I was in town. She was a good person to say the least. I only wish that there were some way to thank her.

Our trips to the library were something else. Patsy always made sure that I would go along with her. It was usually story telling day on the days that we would go. I liked the story telling days because the stories were always told in a family way with everyone listening with all ears catching all the words. She would always tell me that I had to be very quiet at the library because people were there reading and liked their peace and quiet while they were reading. If we were listening to a story we couldn't shout or do anything loud because it would upset the other people there.

The one nice thing about the library was the story telling that the librarians put on each Saturday morning. We would always be sure that we were always on time for the story telling. Sometimes, Story Telling was about someone telling of his or her adventures and at other times the story was read from books. I liked the book reading the most, as did Patsy. She always had a couple of books to bring home too. She would give them to me to carry for her. It made me feel important to carry her books home for her. She would let me carry the books as though I had chosen them myself. It made me feel so proud.

When people would see me with the books they would think that I could read. Which is what Patsy wanted them to think. Of course I didn't mind them thinking that either. Knowing that I couldn't read didn't seem to make any difference. I just let them think that if I could. It made me feel a little bit important, and too, it made Patsy feel the same way I guess. She was always so good to me. She was always looking out for me too. When the other kids were ganging up on me and she was around, she always stepped in and put a stop to the ganging up on me.

Like the one time that I was over on Washington Street and several of the older boys were picking on me. It got worse and worse and pretty soon one of the older boys took a punch at me. Well, I couldn't let that go by without punching him back. So I hauled off and really punch him hard in the face. Well, that's all it took for a real fight to get started. I was doing pretty well for myself and standing up to the older boy quite well I thought, when she steps in with a broom handle and started to hit the older boy with broom handle. Well the kid quit fighting as soon as he saw that she was serious and started to cry because he had been hit. His mother came out of the house to see why her boy was crying and she said that it was good enough for him and to give him another couple of whacks. That settled the fighting right away too.

Another couple of weeks and we would have to go to school for the first time. Gee, time sure goes by in a hurry these days. Seems like just yesterday Ronnie and I were going to the farm for the first time this summer. I got to thinking about time and how it seems to go by us faster than it should.

Who invented time anyhow, I wondered, and why do we have to be thinking all the time about time? My Mother was always saying that it was time to do this or it was time to do that. She had a lot of "times to be doing" for sure even if we were the ones that had "to be doing" the things. Seemed to be an unfair policy to say the least, especially to a small boy. Maybe things would change for the better sometime down the line.

Patsy would always take me with her especially when she went over to Audrey and Delores' house. They were two of our best friends, who lived on the corner of 1st Avenue and Lincoln Street just down the block from us at the store. I, of course, liked that a great deal. Audrey and Delores were the best friends that we had living right near us. They would play with us at almost anything we wanted to do. They had an older brother Bobby but he was gone all the time whenever we came over. He and Dale Frisk from up on the 2nd Avenue end of the block were always gone somewhere together.

Audrey and Delores would take us over to Mrs. St. Jules house for a visit and we would have a ball. Mrs. St. Jules was half tipsy most of the time on vanilla extract that she came into the store to buy. While there the girls would pitch in getting her chores done for her, and I did too. She was especially happy when we would come over in the fall of the year so we could help her with the storm windows. The girls were always happy to have me along to do the heavy lifting like the storm windows. It got so that I was getting pretty good at putting up the storm windows, at least on the ground floor level, but not on the upstairs because I would have to have a ladder.

Patsy was always very good to me. She would take me down to McPhails Ice Cream store at the corner of 3rd Avenue and Lincoln Street whenever she went. We'd always stop there long enough to have a sundae and Mr. McPhail was always glad to see us come in. He'd say, "What shall it be today, Patsy? Chocolate Sundae or Strawberry. And what about the little guy with you?" Then to me he would say, "What would you like today, son?" I, of course, would always say, "Please give me a plain sundae, Archie."

So he would fix up our sundaes and put nuts on them and give them to us. Then he would say, "What else can I do for you?" Patsy would ask him to fix up a cone or whatever for Grandma and the girls at the store. Then it was my job to get the cones or ice cream bars up the hill and down to the store before they melted. So away I'd run all the way to the store, two blocks away.

Patsy was always kind to me in every way. She made me feel great whenever I was with her. She made me very proud to be her brother. She'd always say, "Don't forget Joey either." when someone offered her a drink or something to eat. We were over by The Oliver Mining Shops one day when one of the men asked if she wanted a drink and she said, "Sure, and don't forget about Joey here," and would point to me.

Ronnie was another person that I was always proud to be with. He was there with me always at the farm and was interested in most of the things that I was interested in. He would always want to do the things that I liked to do. When we would go out hunting he would be right there ready to go at the drop of a hat. He was a good shot with the rifle and seldom missed what he shot at, the crows being the basic exception.

Gee, but it was nice to have him along. He was always willing to do the things that I liked to do. He was always there when I needed him for something or other. He was always willing to go anywhere that I wanted to go. Like the time we were on the farm in the spring of the year and we were out of the house walking at night.

We were walking along the trace when we saw something up ahead a little ways. We immediately took off after it. Wouldn't you know it was a skunk that we were chasing? The skunk took it so long and then it let go with a volley of stink that was real stinking badly and it caught Ronnie in the face and all over the front of his jacket. That was about the end of our walk for the night. We headed right back to the farm where we got out of the soiled clothes and into some pajamas.

He was always close by and suggested things for us to do. One day he suggested that we go down to the tomato patch by the big hill just to see how the tomatoes were doing. We went down there and found a snake in amongst the plants. I got a hoe and proceeded to chop it in half but not before I missed the first time that I swung at it. As I say he was a good shot with the 22 and got his share of the woodchucks.

But more than that he had a good sense of humor about him that always stuck out. He was always smiling whenever we were doing something together. I couldn't have wanted a better companion for me at the farm or in town. We slept together in the same rooms at both places and were up and doing things together every day early it seems. Without fail we would be up and outside from the store just as soon as we had awakened. Always looking for something to do.

He was always suggesting things for us to do, like the time he suggested that we go up to John Arcos place to look around to see if there were any varmints around, and when we got up there he spotted a couple of crows just sitting in a branch of a poplar tree just waiting to be shot. Ronnie lifted up the 22 to sight on the two crows and then he waited for the two birds to get in line of his sight. Then he shot, and the two birds fell out of the tree, dead. Then he gave the 22 to me and said for me to go over and see if they were both dead. So I went over to where the two crows lay and picked them both up by their feet and both were deader than dead.

We then heard some noise coming from beyond the woods on the other side of John Arcos place. It sounded like a bunch of kids playing at some sort of game. We went over by the edge of the woods to see what was going on. We were surprised to see bout seven or eight kids playing tag or some such game between the house and the garage building that stood there. We didn't think it would be too smart to get involved with them just yet. So we backed off and made our way back to the farm, after picking up the two crows, of course to show Grandpa what good shots we were. That is what a good shot Ronnie was.

It never seemed like we were idle much of the time. Like when we started doing the chores for the chicken coop. At first it seemed to take up our whole day but then Grandpa came along with us and showed us how and what to do. After that we were doing things fairly well. Getting the feed for the chickens and the new straw for their nests. Even in picking up all the eggs, we were getting good at the game so to speak. With Ronnie along it was always seemed a game sort of thing that we played at every day.

With Ronnie along it never seemed to be a chore, but rather a fun thing to be doing. He always made it seem as though we were out on a hunt or something else that we liked to do. He never ever stood in my way at doing something. Like the time we were down across the main trace at the farm house that stood there all alone. There never seemed to be anyone there at all. This particular day there seemed like there was no one around, and we went up to the window and looked in. There was a girl in a chair by the fireplace, just sitting there looking the other way and she didn't see us until she suddenly turned the chair around. She was looking right at us then, and couldn't help but to see us.

She called out to us to come in by the doorway. So we went over to the doorway on the other end of the house and knocked on the door. She said for us to come in so we did. When she saw the gun she got real shook up bad and wanted us to leave it outside the house. Well Ronnie said that it wasn't loaded but she still wanted us to leave it outside the doorway. So Ronnie put the 22 outside the doorway and came back into the room. She seemed to be a nice sort of girl and was wondering where we came from. Ronnie said that we were from across the road at the Catterini farm. She and Ronnie and I got along quite well, and then she asked if she could come over and meet our Grandma and Grandpa some day. Of course we said, "Yes, you sure can, the very next time that Grandma was at the farm."

Seems as though Ronnie was always there when I needed him, like that day. I would have been all tongue tied up trying to get an answer out of the girl. As it was, Ronnie answered her right straight out right, to each of her questions. He was very good at answering questions from just about everyone. He was such a pleasure to have along all the time. I didn't know what I would have done or said to anyone without his help in being there. He was the greatest guy.

He was always trying to be the first at anything we were doing. He just hated to come in last at running or throwing a ball or anything that we would be doing. We were always competing with each other at everything from running up a hill to washing the car. Grandpa was particularly pleased to have us wash the car and would get the pails of soapy water for us whenever we wanted to wash the car. It would be fun to race with one another to see which one got his side done first. Some times he won and other times I won.

He was always ready to go with me wherever I wanted to go. Like the time that I wanted to walk down the creek bed all the way to Dupont Lake. We just started out one morning to walk along the creek bed and kept on going and going until we got down by Dupont Lake. When we got close enough we could see that all the land was under water in a large swampy area. Well I said that we had better not go any farther and we turned around and went on the way back. When we had gotten to Louie Galots' place we decided to get on the trace that came into his place. So we cut across from the creek to the trace up on the hill.

About then old Louie came out of his house and saw us and called out to us to wait a minute. So we waited a minute and old Louie came over to us and wanted to know just whom we were and where we had come from. So Ronnie starts in telling him that were the two boys from the Catterini farm just up the valley a little ways. He said, "Well I'll just walk with you on your way back to the farm." So he did just that and came walking with us all the way back to the farm. When we got there he said to call your Grandpa for him.

We did and pretty soon here came Grandpa out of the barn and came over to us and said "Hello, Louie. How are you doing?" "Well," Louie says, "I'm doing great but are these two young boys yours?" "Yes they are," said Grandpa. "Why do you ask?" "Well they were down around the creek bed that runs through my place and they said that they belonged here," said Louie. "That's right," Grandpa said, "Were they making any trouble for you, Louie?" "No they were just walking through," said Louie. "Well come and have a glass of vino with me," Said Grandpa. So the two of them went into the little house and had a glass of vino.

Ronnie and I just stayed outside and went over to the chicken coop to start in our chores. It was Ronnie's idea that we get started on the work and we went over to the coop. We had gotten the feed for the birds and were beginning to pick up all the eggs for the day. We had enough for three trips to the little house and started in taking the eggs over to the little house. We made one trip over there with our pockets full along with our arms full and were coming back for another load. Then we took that load over to the little house and came back for the third load. So we loaded up the third load and went over to the little house to start the cleaning.

Ronnie was there for me all through the day. Gee was it ever nice having him there to be doing things with all the time.

Milk for the Deer

The very next day I was on the farm again to see about the deer. Sure enough she was right where we had left her, in the cage with the gate still open. She was just lying there with her head down and not doing anything in particular. When she saw me she got to her feet and came over to the gate to meet me. She didn't even come out of the cage. She just came over to the gateway to say hi. Was I ever happy. Wow! I'd have to remember this for sure to tell Ronnie about it when I wrote to him. It seemed like Spike had done a good job when he watched her the other day. It could be that she was only scared a little bit, but whatever, she just stayed in the cage and didn't come out at all.

At any rate, that was all right with me. I'd just as soon not have her get out of the cage on her own than to have to wonder where she was all the time. I left her where she was and went out to pick some green grass for her and to stop and get her some more bran. She seemed to be quite pleased with both of my choices for her. She bent her little head down and was eating away like it had been declared illegal. I just went over to where she was eating and began to pet her back. She seemed to like that petting better than anything and I kept it up for as long as she was eating.

In a few more minutes she was done and then she surprised me like all get out. She came over to me and licked my face. You could have knocked me over with a feather. I put my arms around her and held her real tight. She didn't seem to mind at all. Then I thought that I would give her some exercise and I took her out of the cage with the little rope that we had placed around her neck the other day. When we had gotten to the field just to the east of where her cage was, there was Grandpa watching us. When I saw him the idea came to me that we should try her on a nipple with some milk. I said so to Grandpa and he agreed that it would probably be a good idea. Grandpa started to walk down to the little house.

We just tagged along with him, me just walking along and the deer was walking with me by my side without a rope of any kind around her neck. Just walking along as though she did it every day with her head held high. Grandpa took a look and said he didn't believe that for sure. He just kept on walking and smiling, shaking his head, not believing any of this. Pretty soon we were at the little house and Grandpa went in to get the nipple and a bottle. Next he went down to the basement to where the milk was kept to keep it cool, and filled the bottle with milk. Then he put the nipple onto the bottle, while the deer and I were coming into the basement. The deer didn't seem to like the idea of the basement too much but she came along looking in all directions for the boogey man I guess. Then Grandpa said that I should feed her the milk and he gave me the bottle. I took the bottle and turned to the deer and said, "Come here." She gave me a look and then she came over to where I was sitting down. I felt certain that she had understood me.

I told Grandpa that the milk was cold, but Grandpa didn't seem to understand what I was saying. I told him that when the milk comes out of the cow's body it was warm. Then Grandpa said, "That's right. Give me the bottle." And he went up stairs of the little house to warm it up. It took him a couple of minutes and soon he was back down in the basement with the deer and I. He gave me the bottle again and said that I should feed her while I held her. I took her in my arms and started to feed her. But she didn't like that a bit and wanted to get down on her legs. I guess that it was feeding instinct that was talking then. When I set her down she came right up to the bottle and took the nipple in her mouth. She drank for all she was worth and when the bottle was empty she put her head over my way and let out another whimper. With that Grandpa took the bottle and refilled it and then went up stairs to heat it up.

This time Grandpa kept the bottle and was going to feed her himself. The deer didn't like the idea too much and held back from going to him even when he put the bottle out toward her. Grandpa kept the bottle, held out to her, and she finally got the idea. She had put all reservations out to pasture and walked over to him. She stood there and drank all the milk that was in the bottle and then came over to me as if to say, "I'm ready." Grandpa said that now the deer would be all right with the two of us, and he said, "Let's go." Up the entrance way we went into the sunshine of the day.

With that accomplished I walked up the hill where her cage was, intending to put her in the cage and shut the gate. When we got up there she entered the cage as if she had always lived there, went over to the pile of hay that we had put in one corner and promptly lay down. It was all just as though it was supposed to be. That's all there was to it, and she was sound asleep within a minute.

One Shot, Two Dead Crows

I went down and told Grandpa that I was going hunting. He said, "All right, but be back in time for supper." I said I would and got the 22 and some bullets and started out. I went out on the trail up to John Arco's place, and didn't see any crows around at all. Maybe they had gotten the word when Ronnie and I were up here last weekend, but I was sure that they would be back soon anyway. Today, it first appeared that not much was happening, but as I approached, I could hear voices just like the last time when Ronnie and I were up here. I stopped to listen to see if I could tell where they were coming from. They were kids voices and seemed to be coming from up ahead some place. I was real curious now, so I got a little closer to the noise.

From where I was now, I could see part of a house and what looked like a garage building next to it. This was very interesting to say the least. I moved in a little closer to the noise. When I did, I could see that there were some kids up ahead who were playing by the house. It looked like a nice house and it was bigger than the little house that we had at the farm. The kids all seemed to be about age of five to ten or so, boys and girls. I couldn't figure out who they were. I sat down there in the woods and simply watched them. As I sat there watching them at play, a woman came out of the house and started speaking in a foreign language that I didn't recognize at all. What in the world was the language that she was speaking? It was totally foreign to me but sounded somewhat like I'd heard it before some place.

Could it be the Croatian language that she was speaking? No, I decided that it was some other kind of language. Maybe it was even the Finnish language. Heaven forbid! She seemed to be telling all the kids to be a little quieter because their father was asleep in the house after his working nights at the mine. They began to play a little quieter and then the woman went back into the house.

I didn't think that I should go in where the children were playing at all, so I picked up the gun and started to walk away. All of a sudden I heard a shout from the direction of the kids. I turned back around. There was a car coming up driveway road of the farm. The kids all gathered around the car and I couldn't see just who it was. I again started to be off on my merry way.

This time, going back to the farm, I went past John Arco's house to see if he was home. When I got close to the house I could see that a car was there in the driveway, so maybe John Arco was there after all. Sure enough, when I got a little closer to the house, I could see him in the yard by his car. I went up to him and said, "Hello. Do you know anything about the kids that were playing at the house just outside the woods?" He replied, "Of course I know them. I think that their name is Peltonon or something like that." I asked, "Are they Finish?" He replied, "Yes, they are Finish, for sure. But that's all I know. You'll have to ask them yourself if you want to know more. What are you doing roaming around on my property?" I told him, "I just come up from our farm down in the valley, hunting." He let out a hoot and a holler about that right when I said hunting. He asked, "Don't you know that we are all on a game preserve and that no hunting was allowed?" I said, "Yes, of course I knew." He asked, "Did you shoot anything?" "Yes, I shot some woodchucks," I said. He smiled and said, "I won't say anything if you won't." I kind of laughed about that and said, "I won't tell a living soul about shooting the woodchucks." Then he started to tell me about the kids at the farm that I had seen. He said, "As far as I know, all of them are good kids and they wouldn't mind it if you dropped in and visited them someday." That was all nice and cozy but not today for sure. I said, "I have to get back to the farm now." I didn't really know why I had to get back to the farm; I just said that to make some conversation.

With that I left Mr. John Arco and headed in the general direction of the farm. On the way, I spotted a pair of crows sitting in a dead tree. I decided to take a shot at them. I loaded the 22 and raised it up to sight the two birds. While I was sighting, one bird stepped in front of the other. This will make a great shot I said and took a good aim and fired the gun. I looked up and the two birds were nowhere to be seen. I walked over to the tree that they had been in to see if I had hit them or not. Gee whiz. There they both were on the ground looking as dead as could be. What a surprise that was! I quickly went over to them to see if they were dead or not. Sure enough, they were both as dead as could be. Too bad Ronnie wasn't here to see this. I'd have to tell him about what a shot I had turned out to be. I picked up the two birds, and went on my way back to the farm.

When I got there no one was around. They must be off somewhere doing something or other. I went up to the cage to see how she was getting along. She was standing up in her cage with the gate open just as I had left her. She seemed happy to see me, and came right over to me. I took her in my arms and held her for a while. She seemed to like that enough but when she saw the two dead crows she became a little excited and wriggled around in my arms like she wanted to get down. I put her down and she went immediately over to where I set the two birds down to smell them. I was at a loss to try to explain this action at all. I just stood there and watched what she was doing. Pretty quick she came over to me and looked at me with those two big beautiful eyes, and let out a whimper as if to say, "What have you done?"

What was I supposed to say or do? I couldn't make excuses to her, she just wouldn't understand. I took the two birds and set them in front of the little house door for Grandpa to see. Then I went back up to where the deer was. Then I thought that I still had the 22 with me so I went on back to the little house and put the gun away. Then I turned around at the door and there was the little deer following me. She scared me out of a year's growth, that's for sure. What was I to do with her, I said to myself. She always seemed to want to be with me. That was sure comforting to know, but what was I to do with her when I wasn't around? I guess that I would just have to leave her in the cage with gate closed until I got back, and that is where I left it for the time being.

I went down to the little house to have supper. Grandpa was just starting supper and I got to set up the dishes and the silverware. Soon I was done with those chores. I said, "I saw some Finish kids at the house beyond John Arco's farm. Grandpa was very inquisitive about them. He asked, "Did you go over to meet them? When I said, "No, I hadn't," he said, "That's good." He left it at that, with me hanging onto thin air wondering why he said it.

We had our supper and were just cleaning up afterwards. Then I decided to lie down on my bed mattress. Grandpa was occupied with reading the Italian paper. Grandpa asked, "Are you feeling sick?" I said, "No, I just wanted to lay down." And pretty soon I was asleep.

The next morning I got up early and went over to the chicken coop to look after the birds. I put on my overalls with the big pockets in them and got out the door and over to the chicken coop early. When I got there I found all the chickens perched up on the rafters and I couldn't figure that one out at all. What were all the chickens doing up there? Surely there is a reason for this weird behavior. It has to be something weird for sure I thought. I went out to get the hay for their nests. Then I started to pick up the eggs. I got enough eggs to fill all my big pockets in the jeans and left the chicken coop to take them over to the little house. When I got back for the rest of the eggs I found that I couldn't carry all of them. I took the ones in the second load over to the little house and came right back to get the rest of the eggs. By using my arms to carry some of the eggs as well as my pockets I was able to carry all the rest of the eggs over to the house. Then I came right back to the chicken coop, to see if I could figure out why all the chickens were up on the rafters.

There on the floor of the chicken coop was an animal that looked somewhat like a rat but I couldn't say for sure what it was. I just chased it out the door and across the yard. I wished to heck that I had had the 22 along with me and then I could have shot him for sure. As it was, he was up on the hill where the old house had stood, gone in the brush and was gone for sure. Never the less, I vowed to bring the 22 over with me tomorrow morning just in case he came around again. With that I just sat down on some hay to spend the day with the chickens. Grandpa said, "Go get some bran and green grass for the deer." I had almost forgotten about her in the excitement at the chicken coop. Off I went for the cage on the hill by the new house.

It isn't often in this life that we are presented with a happy, happy moment. This was one of those times, for sure. When I got up to the deer's cage, I found the gate had been left open and the deer was nowhere to be seen. I looked all over the cage and then I finally found her. She had burrowed herself under the hay in the corner of the cage, and was there sound asleep. I had thought that she had left the cage and had gone out on her own. When I found her all asleep under the hay I was quite surprised, to speak without fear of contradiction. She was just sleeping there with no fears at all. Soon she awakened and then got up and came over to me where I was sitting. She reached up and licked my face. I was so surprised that I let out a little noise. She immediately drew away from me, but I reached for her and she came right to me again.

Then I said out loud, "Let's go get some grass for you," and started out of the cage. She didn't seem to want to come outside with me. I bent over and fetched the rope that we had used for her neck. Then I turned toward her and she came right over to me and let me put the rope around her neck. With that she seemed to want to go outside the cage. I said, "OK. Let's go." and started for the gate with her right behind me. When we got outside of the cage she put her two front feet down on the ground hard and stiff legged. She didn't seem to want to go out to the field where I was heading. When I stepped back to her, she turned toward the little house and made a step or two in that direction.

Then it came to me that she wanted some more milk. I took the hint that she had given me and started down the hill toward the little house. She seemed happier than all get out about that move and off we loped to the little house. When we got there she stayed outside while I went in to the basement and got her a bottle of milk. Then upstairs I came and went into the house to warm up the milk. Grandpa was sitting in there and he said, "Where are you going with the bottle of milk?" I said, "To warm it up a little." Then Grandpa came over to the stove and showed me what to do. All this time the deer had been peacefully waiting outside the house, so I went over to the door and said, "Come." She came into the house just as if she understood every word of what we were saying. I was so proud of her that minute!

Next thing I new the milk was warm enough for her to drink so I went over to sit down on a chair and she followed me. I held the bottle while she drank all the milk. She eagerly looked for more milk. Down I went to get her another bottle of milk. Then upstairs I went again to heat it up a little. I turned around and gave her the bottle and she ate away happy as could be. When she had finished I said, "Let's go get you some green grass." I started for the door with the deer right behind me. This time though I didn't put the rope around her neck just to see what she would do.

She followed me out the door and into the yard very calmly. When we were out there I said to her, "Eat some grass." At first she didn't seem to want any. I got down on my all fours with my head to the ground and my face down in the grass. She looked at me like I was crazy, or at least that's what I thought. I came up with my head and a mouthful of grass so she would get the idea. It seems like that was all I had to do, because then she started to eat the grass too. In fact she was eating the grass like it was going out of style for sure.

After a little while she quit eating the grass and came over by me and was just standing there, looking around at the buildings. When she had had her fill of the buildings she started up the hill toward the cage, and all by herself she went into the cage and lay down on the hay in the corner, and went to sleep. I said to Grandpa, "Let's leave her there and see what she does." He said, "OK."

We started talking about the kids that I had seen earlier today and that I would like to know more. He said that so would he, with a far away look in his eye. He said that we should go look for ourselves and that right now would be a fine time to go. With that he started walking over to the chicken coop. I was wondering why he went over to the chicken coop, and I said so to him. He just gave me a look that said, "You imbecile. Don't you know anything at all?" and kept on walking toward John Arco's place. It's nice that he took that route because it showed me a new way to get up there. I had been going past the chicken coop without turning left to go right by it. I had been going on by the left turn and on past the hill where the old house had been and then turning left to go past the hill.

John Arco's place was empty when we went by it so we didn't stop there at all. We just kept going until we got close to the house and could hear the kids out playing again like they were the other time I was up here. When we got close enough to see them we stopped and just watched. Pretty quick the mother came out and said something in that foreign language again and then went back inside. We had been there about a half hour when Grandpa looked at his watch and said it was getting late and that we had better go. Off we went back the way we had come.

When we got by the chicken coop again Grandpa said that we should stop in for a minute. When we opened the door there were all the chickens up on the rafters again and there was the varmint, the rat-like animal on the floor looking up at them. Grandpa saw him and let out a holler that would have scared even someone that was used to hearing him holler. It even scared me it was so loud. The animal took off at a high rate of speed, out the door he went and we didn't see him again. The birds stayed up on their roosting places so I went out to get hay for the nests. When I had done that I looked for the eggs and picked up a couple of pockets full and left to carry them over to the house. With that chore done I looked around for a basket to carry the eggs in and found one that was just the right size. I took it back to the chicken coop to get the rest of the eggs. I found that Grandpa had gotten feed for the birds and was waiting for the last two to come down form their perch. I just went around to the nests and collected the rest of the eggs, putting them in the basket. When I had finished picking up the eggs we left for the little house.

Just as we left the chicken coop we spotted the varmint in the grass near the coop. I said to Grandpa, "I'll go get the 22," and started running for all I was worth over to the house. I got the 22 and hurried back to the coop. Grandpa was still there watching the animal when I arrived. He said to give him the gun so I did. He raised the gun up to sight it on the varmint. He had it in his sights and then he pulled the trigger.

Oh what the heck! The gun didn't fire, and the varmint ran away up the hill! Grandpa was all in an uproar and wanted to know why the gun hadn't fired! That's easy. He looked in the chamber. I hadn't even put a shell in it! I hadn't even remembered to stop long enough to pick up the bullets! How dumb could a person get? I guess I was the dumbest of the dumb! Grandpa just stood there and stared at me sternly. In about ten minutes or so he started to laugh, and he laughed loud and long. He soon had me laughing too! We laughed and laughed about "there weren't any shells" in the gun! It was so stupid of me that it was indeed funny! With that, he sent me back to the house to get some bullets. When I got back he said for me to stay at the coop and keep my eyes open for the varmint. Then he went back to work on his chores.

To make a long story shorter, I did stay at the coop for the rest of the day. The varmint didn't show itself at all, all day. Grandpa came over about five o'clock and wanted to know if I was interested in eating. I was so hungry that I shouted, "YES!" and then he said to come on over to the house to eat. Grandpa had made our supper all nice even before his afternoon milking chore. I knew right then why I loved my Grandpa so much.

We were seated down eating when suddenly there was a kind of tapping across the room by the doorway. I turned around and there was the little deer looking so forlorn and lost. She came right over to me and licked my face. I said, "We miss you too little one". I went and got some bran for her to eat and gave it to her. She seemed to like that well enough and started in eating it. Grandpa and I went on with our supper and when we were done, the little deer was done also. I then went outside with the little deer close behind me and I went down the basement to get her some milk. When I came up she was just dancing around. Showing me how happy she was with me, and the milk. I went upstairs to warm the milk a little and she followed me in. When the milk was ready I took it out on the porch by the stairs. She came right along but she wanted to stay on the porch while she drank her milk. That was OK with me so I fed her the milk and when it was gone I went down the basement for a second bottle for her. After going upstairs to warm it up a little, I came out to the porch again and fed her the second bottle.

I sat there looking at her and wondered if she was growing some or just putting on some weight. I couldn't decide which, so I didn't think about it any more. After she finished with the bottle, it was time for her to go back up to her cage and she started right out doing just that. I couldn't be prouder of her than if she had a brain of her own! What a wonderful day this was turning out to be! Just to check on her I went up the hill to the cage. She was there, all right. Just settling down for a little shut eye on the hay and when saw me she came over to me and leaned against my leg. I said to her, "You know that you can stay for as long as you want, but soon you will feel the urge to leave here. That will be all right with us. You can leave any time you wish. But please come back once in a while to see us." She stepped back and looked at me as if to say, "Are you telling me to get out?" She just stayed right where she was and looked at me with those big, beautiful eyes, with a look that said, "I don't want to go any where."

I got to thinking about the varmint over in the chicken coop. Down the hill to the little house I went to get the 22, and some shells this time. Then I meandered over to the chicken coop. I even remembered to load the 22 with a shell. When I got close to the coop I caught a glimpse of him sneaking into the coop. He seemed to be using a hole in the wall and I decided that I would put a rock in the hole later. In the meantime I went immediately into the coop. There he was on the floor in front of the nests, just licking his chops for sure. I lifted up the 22, took a sighting, and shot. The varmint was over on his back, deader than a doornail. I immediately went over to it and looked at it closely. It sure looked like a varmint to me. The chickens all seemed to know that he was dead and began to come down from the rafters and look also. I went out to find a couple of sticks so I could carry him over to let Grandpa see it too. I got some sticks and came back into the coop to get the varmint, and was met by a greeting of loud clucks from all the birds in the coop. I took the two sticks and picked up the varmint and started out the door to go over and show grandpa. When I got outside the coop I just caught a glimpse of another animal running to the hill and the brush. So, I said that I had better see about plugging up the hole in the wall of the coop.

I put the animal and the sticks down first. Then I went over to the wall where I had seen the varmint trying to get in. Sure enough there was a small hole in the wall, but it wasn't at ground level. It was about six inches above the ground and small enough to stop a varmint that big, or so I thought. It would need a board of some six inches or so long, nailed in the place to stop any more from getting in. I went back and picked up the varmint and started out for Grandpa again. When I got across the creek again I went into the barn with the varmint. You would have thought that I was bringing in a live snake or some such, for all the noise that the cows made. Grandpa said for me to get the heck out of there, right away. Outside I went, dead animal and all, and left the darned varmint out there, and then I went back in to tell Grandpa about the hole in the wall of the chicken coop. He was still in the midst of his milking chore and said for me to wait a little.

When he was all done milking he said for me to come along with him to the little house, so I tagged along. When he got the milk put away, he said, "Now what is the matter?" I told him about the hole in the wall of the chicken coop and said that we would need a board of about six inches square or more to cover it up to keep the other varmints out. He agreed but maybe something else was necessary as well, and he would take a look at it in the morning. That seemed good enough to me and I said so. I just left it at that and didn't think any more about it.

The next morning we had all the morning chores to do and were busy doing them. After I had seen to the little deer, I got the 22 and some bullets. Then I started out for the chicken coop. When I got over there I saw another varmint like the last one in the yard of the coop. I lifted up the 22 and shot at him, but I had missed him. He took off for the hill at a high rate of speed. This was getting to be a real problem. Every time we turned around there was another varmint it seemed. That was all right except that we still had to seal up the hole in the wall. Just about then Grandpa was coming over to the coop, and he shouted, "What are you shooting at?" I told him about the other varmint being there and how I had missed him and he had gone up the hill.

Grandpa had a board and some nails and wanted to know where the hole in the coop was. I showed him and he said that a board would be all right for a couple days but that we would have to do something else by then. We nailed the small board over the little hole, and went into the coop to get the eggs. All the birds were up on the rafters and were cackling away like crazy. They all seemed glad to see us and started to come down. In the meantime, I went around to the nests and started to pick up the eggs using the basket. I had gotten about three quarters of the way around, when I found a broken egg. I told Grandpa about it and he came over and cleaned it up right away. I then finished up collecting the eggs and took them over to the little house. I came right back to the coop and then I asked Grandpa what he had meant about having to do something else to the walls of the coop. He said that if the walls were rotting out near the bottom we would have to cement them up about four feet or so.

That seemed like a lot of work but he said that I could do it. I wanted to know how we could do the job. He replied that all we had to do was to get a cement mixing boat and start in on the job. I said that I didn't know what a cement boat was let alone know how to mix the plaster up. He said he would show me just what to do to make up the plaster and how to put it on the coop. With that we went back to the little house so I could wash up the eggs and put them into cartons.

When we got over by the house here comes the little deer down the hill with Spike the dog loping along beside her. Another real surprise, it was, to find the two of them getting along so well and coming down to see us. I kept on going into the house to begin cleaning the eggs up. When I had finished up the cleaning job I began to put them into cartons ready to take to the store. Then it was time to greet our little friend and see if she was all right since the last time I saw her. I took her some bran and got a bottle of milk fixed up for her also. I put the bottle of milk up on the stove to heat up in the pan of water that I also had there. Soon the bottle was ready and I took it to the little deer. She just drank it down like there was no tomorrow. After she was done, she went out to the grass and ate some more lunch. Soon she started up the hill to the cage. I just sat there and watched her go.

When I was sure that she had gotten to the cage I stopped watching her and went to get the 22 again, with some more bullets this time. I started out for the mound of woodchucks up by the railroad track. When I had gotten to the top of the grain shed hill good old dependable Spike came running up to me and seemed to want to go along. I said, "Come along Spike." and he did. Of course he was running all over the place in his happiness and barking quite a bit. Those two antics of his would scare any woodchucks that might have been out on the mound. But I went up there just in case one might be out and hadn't heard Spike. No such luck. The mound was completely clean of woodchucks and I decided to go up the potato hill to look around up there. I told Spike to be quiet and started up to the potato hill the back way.

We were walking through the pasture area and having a grand old time, when Spike took up his pointing stance. I became a little curious as to why he was pointing. I looked ahead as much as I could, but I didn't see a thing. I stood there for a while and let Spike do his posing. After about ten minutes or so he took himself out of the pointing position and returned his normal self. Pretty soon we came to the back of the potato patch and Spike was very quiet indeed. He seemed to know why we were here and didn't bark at all. We walked along the North edge of the field and kept on watching for the woodchucks all the time. We didn't see a one out in the field or over by their den. This got me to wondering about it for sure. We went over to the den site to look it over.

There wasn't one chuck to be seen there either. We went over to the den holes and looked in them. There were the two chucks that we had shot the other day still in the holes were we had put them and not a sign of the rest of the chucks. Maybe we had done some good by stuffing the two dead chucks into their holes. We felt pretty happy about that. I called it a day and started down the hill and back toward the house. We had gotten to the bottom of the hill at the haunted woods place, and I decided to go into the woods. This was all well and good with Spike and he came along for the excursion into the haunted woods. When we had gotten about ten yards into the woods Spike came up to his pointing stance and stood there looking towards the far side of the woods. He was very stiff and quiet. I looked and looked but I couldn't see a thing that I thought might interest him in the least. Then all of a sudden a rabbit hopped his way out of the woods on the far side and Spike took off at a full run. After the rabbit he was.

My New Friend, the Rabbit

The rabbit had a good start on him but that didn't seem to make much of a difference to Spike. He just ran after the rabbit for all he was worth. I just stood there and watched the show. Soon, Spike caught the rabbit. Only he didn't kill it. He just kind of held it in his paws and looked at it for a while. I walked up the hill to where he was for a better look. Then he reached over and grabbed the rabbit in his mouth and started off toward the cage where the little deer was. I was flabbergasted to say the least! I went along to see just what he had in his mind about the rabbit. Soon he was at the cage. He went into the cage and he let the rabbit out of his jaws. Then he just stood there and watched the rabbit and the deer look and smell each other. That's all it took. The deer made out with her little cooing noises and the rabbit just stood there. Spike went over by the cage door and sat down to watch the whole proceeding. When he was satisfied that the two of them knew each other, he left us just standing there and went down to the little house.

I closed the door to the cage because I was afraid that the rabbit would run away for sure if I didn't close up the cage. Spike was sitting over by the new house watching all of us like a guard. When I came over by him, he came to me wagging his tail like he approved of everything I'd done. That was good to see, to say the least. It probably meant that I had finally been accepted as one of the gang. I couldn't have felt any prouder than I did then! I went down to get them bran and Spike trotted along with his head held high just as if he owned the whole darned farm. On the way back I picked quite a bit of green grass. When I had all my pockets full I went on to the cage and opened the gate to go in, and both the deer and the rabbit just watched me as I unloaded my pockets and the put the bran down on the ground for them. The deer was the first one to come over to the bran, and was standing eating. Then she looked up in the direction of the rabbit, and gave a little noise. That was all it took. The rabbit came over to the bran and started to eat some. There was all the grass to eat too, so I closed the cage again, and I went on down to the little house.

When I got down to the little house there was spike walking around with his tail wagging just strutting up a storm. Good old Spike. He was always trying to win my favor with his walking and strutting around. This time he did just that, and I went over to the steps into the little house to sit down and he came along with me. He sat down next to me and I started to scratch him behind his ears a little. He liked that a lot that's for sure and just sat there for as long as I wanted to scratch him.

It didn't take long before the rabbit was acclimated to the pen and before I knew it she was hopping all over the place. Whenever I came up to the pen from the little house or wherever, she was always hopping around or sleeping. Seems like she did those two things better than anything else. Well she didn't have anything else to do at least not that I was privy to. She got so that she was even happy to see me come up to the pen and was always standing on her back feet whenever I came up to the pen. That was so nice to see and I always stooped down to her to pet her and say hello to her whenever I came up to the pen.

This was letting her know me a little and I to know her a little better each time. Soon we were the best of friends and she always came over to the gate whenever I came there. She had become the best of friends with the deer too. One couldn't go anywhere without the other. If the deer went over to the pile of hay to sleep the rabbit was always right there to get her forty winks in too. Seems like in no time at all the two of them were inseparable.

That was as it should be. The two of them made good friends and enjoyed each other's company. Where ever one went the other was tagging right along. Whatever one did the other did too. If one went over to the hay to sleep the other came right over to the hay to lie down and sleep. They became inseparable friends and were always together. I was at a loss to explain why two animals so different from one another should become such good and fast friends.

That was ok by me as long as they stayed friendly and were with each other and as long as I knew where they were I was happy too. I began to wonder just how long they would stay in the cage at the top of the new house hill before they were gone for good.

It seemed like in no time at all the rabbit became my friend too. In a matter of a couple of weeks she was coming to the gate to meet me when I came up to the pen. She was always looking for something to eat and let me know when she was disappointed that I hadn't brought her something to eat. She would run up to me expecting to be fed whatever I had with me and when she wouldn't find anything to eat she would hop over to the hay and lie down as if she were sleeping. That was always good to see and it told me that she was dependant on me for her food, which is what I wanted, I guess.

She and the little deer got along just perfectly. When one would getup to go somewhere the other would be on her feet too. This was always nice to see because it told me how much they dependant on each other. It also said a great deal about how they felt about each other. There was an entanglement there that was hard to put into words, except that you just knew that they cared for each other an awful lot.

What was nice about her was her getting up her hind legs with her front paws on my leg and stretching out her neck to get a look at me.

She did this every time I'd come into the pen. She didn't do this with any one else which was a bit strange but understandable if you really thought about. She had come to like me I guess, and that's abut that could be said about it.

Spike, on all his wisdom, made a great decision when he brought her over to the cage that day. Another of the fine things that we had to thank Spike for, now if only the three of them would become friendly, we would all be a bit happier. I guess that would come on its' own some day. In the meantime we just had to wait and see I guess. So we settled down to wait and see hoping that it wouldn't be too long in coming.

Fixing Up the Chicken Coop

On Monday I decided to go see what the kids were doing at the house near John Arco's place. I got the 22 and started out, Spike decided to come along with me, to give moral support I guess. I stopped off at the barn to see Grandpa for a little while before I left. I asked him, "When are we going to fix the hole in the chicken coop?" He said, "We could do it almost anytime … today if you like." "Let's do it right now," I said. "OK then, you'll have to go get the cement boat and bring it over to the chicken coop." He then told me what the cement boat looked like so I wouldn't miss it when I looked for it. I went up to the hill where the new house sat waiting to be set on its foundation. Sure enough there was a cement boat just as Grandpa had described. It was much too large for me to carry, and I tried pushing it, and I couldn't do that either.

I went back down to Grandpa and said, "It's too big for me to move. I'm going to need a little help." Grandpa smiled a little and said he would come right up and give me a hand. I said to myself that the kids would have to wait while Grandpa and I fixed up the coop. In a few more minutes Grandpa came up just as he said he would, and he had the team with him. That didn't surprise me in the least. I had figured that the weight of the boat was enough to merit having the team pull it over to the coop. Grandpa said for me to go down the hill and get the wheelbarrow, which I did immediately. I met grandpa coming down the road down the hill with the cement boat in tow. He turned the team toward the shed and soon stopped in front of the shed.

He went into the shed and I followed him. He got a sack of cement left over from making the basement walls, and took it out to the cement boat. He said, "You get another sack of cement." I went over to the shelf where the cement bags were kept and tried to lift one. I just couldn't do it! The cement was just too heavy for me. Grandpa came backing smiling away again. This time he said to me, "It is good to know when not to do a job, too. When something is too heavy for you, don't try to lift it. Get some help." With that said he lifted the sack of cement and took it out to the cement boat. He said that he thought that the two sacks of cement would be enough and we could go over to the coop to get started. We both climbed aboard the boat and sat down on the sacks of cement to ride over to the coop. He gave a little whistle and the team started to go. The ride over to the coop was OK until we came within about fifty yards of the coop. Then we saw a varmint running away from the coop and going up the hill. It's a good thing we were going to fix up the hole in the coop.

Grandpa didn't stop at the coop he kept going over to the sand pit. There he had the team pull us up to the side of the pit. Then he got out of the cement boat and, with a shovel, he started to load up the cement boat with sand. When he had about three quarters of the boat filled he said, "Let's go and make the cement." He then drove the team back to the rear of the coop and parked the boat about ten yards behind the coop. We took a shovel apiece and began to put all of the sand in a pile on the ground. When we got done with that little job, Grandpa said that it was time for lunch. We unhooked the boat from the team and went back to the barn. Grandpa went in to put the team away, and I ran up to the cage to check on my two friends.

Sure enough they were still there and both of them came over to the gate to meet me. I was sure happy about that maneuver. They seemed glad to see me for sure. I opened the gate and left it open for the two of them to come out if they wanted to. I went on down the hill to the little house. I took some bran out for the two of them, thinking that they would soon come on down the hill. I was right, and before another twenty minutes the two of them came down the hill together. Boy was I ever a happy camper. They dug right into the bran and then went across the lawn where there was some nice grass growing and settled down to eating their fill. Meanwhile Grandpa was fixing our lunch so I got cleaned up and sat down to eat. After our lunch I settled in at the sink and started to wash up the dishes. This was a first for me and Grandpa came over to the sink to help me and to give me some pointers on washing dishes.

When we were done with that little chore we went outside and I remembered the varmint that had been there this morning. I quick ran back inside to get the 22 and some bullets. Then over to the coop we went. When we got there. We saw the varmint again leaving the area and going up the hill. We had gotten there a little too late to get a shot at him. That didn't matter. There would be another time I was sure. We then went to the cement boat in the back of the coop, and started making the cement that we would use to fix up the coop. We had gotten one batch mixed up and Grandpa was looking at the building that made up the coop.

He said, "You know, I think we should put the cement on the bottom of the building up to about three feet or so. We started in carrying the cement over to the building and putting it on the place. Man, what a chore that was for sure! It was more than carrying all the water from the creek, and mixing all the cement. I was plain tuckered out, to say the very least. But that was ok by me. I started in putting the cement on the bottom of the building walls. The job was going along just fine when I heard a little noise from the front of the building. I went over to the cement boat to get the 22 and hastily ran around to the front of the building. There was the varmint just standing out in front of the coop like he owned it. I raised the 22 up to my eye and shot him. I went over and grabbed him by the tail and took him out to the back of the building, to show him to Grandpa and he said,

"Good shooting. Now maybe we don't have to put the cement all around the building." I said, "Maybe we do. Because who knows if this was the last of them or not." He agreed with me and went right back to work.

We worked away at the job of cementing the walls up to about three feet the rest of the day. Pretty soon Grandpa said that it was time for supper. We quit work for the day and got our tools all cleaned up. Then we came over to the little house to have our supper. The little deer and the rabbit were nowhere to be seen and I didn't think about it very much. I just assumed that the two of them had gone back to the cage. Grandpa went on with his chore of making supper and soon had it all ready to eat. I was famished and said so. We sat down to eat our supper. When we had finished eating he said that he still had his chores to do so he left to do them. I cleaned and washed our dishes. Then I took the 22 and went over to the chicken coop again.

I didn't see any varmints around anywhere so I went into the coop and looked around and all the birds were up on their roosting poles. Then I saw why. There was a varmint on the floor about halfway between the door and the nests. I popped off a shot at him but I must have been suffering from buck fever because I missed him completely. Before I could get reloaded he was out the door and climbing the hill again. I ran to the door to catch sight of him but he was already up the hill it seemed, and I never saw him again. I only wish that I could go as fast some day. Then I went back inside and remembered that I had not collected the eggs that day at all. I put the 22 down and got out the egg-carrying basket and went around on my egg retrieving duties. I took all the eggs over to the little house and came right back to the coop to get the 22.

Just as I went into the coop via the door, all the birds began to put up an insane cackling. I turned around and looked and sure enough there was a varmint on the floor right by the door. It didn't take any more to get me in shape. I just lifted the 22 and cocked it on the way up to my shoulder, sighted and shot the varmint dead as could be. All that was done within the space of about five seconds or so. Then I went over to the varmint and poked him with the 22 just to make sure he was dead and sure enough he was deader than a doornail. Two varmints was quite a score to say the least. I was proud as a peacock strutting around telling all the birds how good a shot I was. But I couldn't see where he had come in. I went to get a couple of boards to pick up the varmint but I couldn't find any. That meant that I would have to use the next best thing, my hands. I leaned down and picked him up by the tail. With varmint in my clutches I started out to go show Grandpa, and to get his words of praise too.

Grandpa was impressed enough to say a word or two. He and I thought that we should get back on the job of putting cement on the coop walls just as soon as possible. That would be tomorrow morning for sure. Right after breakfast we would be back on the job. Then I called Spike to come over and see my catch. He must have been up at the cage because it took him about twenty minutes to come over to the barn door. When he finally got there he didn't even stop to see what I wanted of him. He just went for the varmint, took it in his mouth and started to shake it rather violently. When he thought that he had done enough he put the varmint down and ran down to the creek to get a drink of water and wash out his mouth. Then he came back up to me and wanted some praise for killing the dead varmint. Didn't that beat all!

I looked around just then and saw the deer and the rabbit coming across the barnyard toward us. I went over to meet them and turned right around and came back to the barn door. They both stopped suddenly when they saw the dead varmint lying there. They wouldn't come a step closer. Then Spike stepped in, to save the day so to speak. He picked up the dead varmint in his mouth and took it over to them to see, laying it down at their feet. Neither of them would even smell the dead varmint at first, but after Spike took it up in his mouth again and shook it quite a bit and the ball game seemed to change for the better. Then the two of them came over to the varmint and smelled it. They just took one little sniff and right away they turned away from the dead varmint.

With that I think it was the end of the day. They all seemed to agree with me and started off for their cage to turn in for the night. Grandpa said that we had a big day in front of us and we should get some sleep. With that I went on up to the cage to see that they got there ok, and then went on to the little house to go to bed.

Morning becomes electric they say, and we were up by 5 o'clock. We had our breakfasts, got the 22, started out the door. The deer and the rabbit were waiting for us to come out. I was more than just happy to see them both. I had to stop and get a bottle ready for the deer and feed it to her, followed by the second bottle. The rabbit spent his getting-up time eating the grass in the yard. When the deer had finished the second bottle, I said goodbye to them and headed out for the chicken coop. Grandpa had gone over there ahead of me and had the first batch of cement ready to be put on the coop walls.

There wasn't any sign of the varmints at all. I figured they were still sleeping … "so much the better." I started putting the cement on the wall of the coop while Grandpa made up some more cement. We worked along until 10:30 or 11:00 when the last of the wall base was covered up to about three and half feet. Then we quit work to inspect our accomplishment. "Good job," said Grandpa, "I never would have found that first hole in the wall by myself. It's a good thing that you are here on the farm with me. Thank you very much." I was astounded. I didn't know what to say. So, I said the first thing that came to mind, "Maybe I should just wait here to see if another varmint comes down the hill." Grandpa said, "OK but don't forget your lunch. I've got to go over and do the milking. The cows are getting noisy about it." With that, he left me sitting in front of the coop and he went over to the barn.

I spotted something up on the hill where the old farmhouse had been. It looked very much like another of the varmints. I just sat still and watched to see where he was going and what he was going to do. I must have watched him about a quarter of an hour when he turned to go back into his house. I was mistaken because here he came down the hill in a couple of more minutes. Then I took up the 22 and just waited for him to get to the bottom of the hill. When he came to the bottom of the hill he saw me sitting there and went to turn around and go back up the hill, but I was ready for him. I already had the 22 up and was sighting. I shot and hit him square. There lay varmint number three. I was happy that I had stayed and went over to the place where the varmint was lying. I picked him up by the tail and took him over to the barn for Grandpa to see. Boy! What a happy day this was turning out to be. Grandpa was all smiles too. Then I just went over to the little house to wait until Grandpa was done with the milking chores. Pretty quick he came over to the little house with the last pail full of milk and went down the basement to pour it into the large milk cans. He then came back upstairs and said, "Its about time for our lunch." With that he went on upstairs to get our lunch ready. I went down to the creek to wash up. I took the bar of Fells Naptha soap to do an extra good job.

When I came back up there were my two friends, the deer and the rabbit waiting for me. I went over and got a shovel full of bran and gave it to them for their lunch. Grandpa had our lunch ready by then so I went up to eat too. After lunch I did the dishes and left them out to dry. I figured to go hunting a little more. I got the 22 and some more bullets and started out for John Arco's place. I hadn't gone ten feet when here comes Spike loping along like there was no tomorrow. I said to him, "Come along Spike, if you are of a mind to." He seemed quite happy with that and off we went. We were following the track that Grandpa had gone on the other day. We had gotten about a half-mile or so when I spotted a crow up ahead a little way. Quietly I went up to the place I had spotted it and looked about. Sure enough, he was in a tree just a little ways ahead of me. I lifted up the 22 and sighted on the crow. Bang went the gun when I pulled the trigger and the crow fell out of the tree.

Wowee! Wasn't this going to be a fine day? Spike immediately ran up to the crow and just stood there looking down at it. I came up there too and looked at the crow on the ground in a heap. I bent over to fetch the bird but spike growled a warning to me and I didn't pick it up right away. Then I could see that it wasn't dead yet. I just left it there and waited awhile. Pretty soon Spike walked over to the crow and picked up in his mouth so I thought for sure it must be dead. It was another prize to take to Grandpa on the way back. I took the crow from Spike and put it on a branch of the tree that was lower down, about five feet or so from the ground. With that taken care of, I went on my way up to John Arcos' place. When I got there, there wasn't a soul around. I kept on going to the farm just past the woods.

I figured that I would let myself be seen, this time. I got up to the little farm and then I thought I'd better not go in there with the 22 for sure. I picked out a tree and placed the 22 leaning up against it, sort of out of sight. Then I told Spike to stay there and watch it for me. He was all in favor of that proposal so I left him there and went on over to the little farm. On the way over there I didn't hear any noise from the kids. I thought that that was sort of strange, but I kept on going just the same. When I got over there I didn't see any kids at all. I went up to the door to the kitchen and knocked on it. Pretty soon a woman came to the door all flustered because someone was knocking on her door. She opened the door and there I stood, a complete stranger to her and just a little boy stranger at that.

I could have knocked her over with a feather that's for sure. She said, "Who are you and what do you want?" I said, "I am Joe McGraw. I came from my Grandpa's farm down in the valley. Where are all the kids?" That just about floored her, I guess. When she got her wits back she said, "My name is Gladys Wirtenen. The kids are all in town getting some new clothes for school. They wouldn't be there at all today." She asked, "What is your name again?" "Joe McGraw, ma'am", and my Grandpa's name is Joseph Catterini." She said that she knew both names and could I come back again some other day. Why yes, I could I said. With that I turned to leave and then she said, "When?" I told her that I couldn't say for sure but I thought that maybe the day after tomorrow would perhaps be all right maybe right after lunch. She said OK and then I turned away and left. I walked quickly to the woods and found Spike sitting right where I had left him under the tree that had the crow in it. I got the crow and the 22 and started off for the farm.

When we got back to the farm, I told Grandpa about my little visit and he was surprised to say the least. Then I went up to see the deer and the rabbit. Both were all right when I got there. In fact they were both sound asleep inside the cage with the dog, Spike, lying by the door to the cage. He was just watching them, I guess, or maybe he was a little bit jealous of them getting most of the attention from me. Anyway, he was there watching out for them, and that's all that counts. I was about done in anyhow and needed to go to sleep myself. I went down to the little house and went in to go to sleep myself.

I must have slept right through supper and the rest of the night, because when I woke up the sun was up and shining from the wrong side of the room. I must have needed the rest, I guess, because I was chipper as can be. Grandpa had been watching me sleep and said, "Do you want some breakfast?" "Sure." I said. Then he said, "Its 10:00 o'clock. Maybe you should wait for lunch." "Oh no!" I said. He said that he had it all ready because he just finished making it, and then he stood there watching me sleep for a little while. With that I got up and got dressed. Then he said to come to the table, which I did and he fed me. He told me that my two friends had come down looking for me while I slept. They came into the house to look at me and the deer smelled my face. I didn't wake up, though. My two friends then went outside to eat some grass and go back to their cage. I just couldn't believe it! I asked him if he had given them any bran or milk. He said that yes, he had.

As a change of pace, I decided to go fishing in the creek. I got the pole with the reel on it and went down to the island. I had a big new lure on the line that I hadn't used yet and I was anxious to try it out. I was standing on the island facing the large pool that the creek had formed there. I cast the lure and line out just about to the other edge of the pool and started reeling it in when suddenly there was a splash of water and a tug on the line. I thought that I had a fish for sure. When I got the line all reeled in there was a fish on the end of it. It wasn't just a small fish either. It was a northern about five or six pounds I guessed. I took the fish up to dry land by the garden and I took out the hook. I took the fish up to Grandpa and showed him. Was he ever surprised to see how big it was! He wanted to weigh it right away. I took the fish to the little house where we had a scale and weighed the fish. It was nine and a half pounds. A nice sized fish anyway you look at it.

Grandpa didn't know how to cook a fish and I didn't know how to clean it! However, he knew how to clean it. He said that Grandma was coming down the day after tomorrow and he could ask her about cooking it. With that problem solved he started to show me how to clean a fish. When that was done we wrapped the meat in waxed paper and put it all in the basement to keep it cool. Then we cleaned up the fish cleanings and got rid of the scraps that were left. With that I went back to my fishing from the island. I began casting for a while, without any bites. I made one last cast up near the rapids and was reeling it in when I had another strike. I thought that this one was as big as the first one was, by the weight that I felt on the line. As I reeled it in I felt that I should just keep the line tight and let him tire himself out with the fighting. When I finally got it in to the island he looked even bigger than the first one that I had caught. I took him up to the dry land by the garden before I took the hook out of his mouth. Then I got a good look at him. Was he ever big! Boy! Oh boy! He'd be at least seven or eight pounds for sure!

I took out the hook and carried him up to weigh him. Thirteen pounds! Thirteen pounds! That was a record for sure! I took him up to grandpa and showed him, too. Was I ever proud! You could have let me march in the parade all day! Wow! I was just strutting my stuff all the way up town and back. I had caught a fish that weighed 13 pounds, what do you know about that! Grandpa was also proud and happy that I caught it. My! Oh my! What a wonderful day this was turning into! Now all I had to do was to thank the Good Lord for the day, which I had been doing ever since I pulled the big fish in. Then Grandpa suggested that we fillet the two fish and give them to Grandma to sell in the store. I said, "Sure enough!"

With that he said that we should best stop and eat something for our lunch. While Grandpa was in fixing our lunch I went up to the cage to see my two friends. I found the two of them still inside the cage just lazing the day away. After petting and hugging them both, I said for them to come with me down to the little house, which they seemed more than willing to do. When we got there I found the Grandpa had made our lunch and was serving it out for the two of us. I sat down to eat and then the rabbit came over to me and sat down at my foot. He put his paws up on my leg and looked at me as if to say, "Where's our lunch?"

With that, I couldn't hold out any more. I just had to get down from my chair and go get them some bran so they could eat a little too. With that little chore out of the way I went back to my chair and finished eating. Then the little deer came over to me as if to say, "Where's my milk?" I got down from my chair and went down stairs to get the first bottle of milk. I started going back up when I said to myself, "Why don't you get another bottle fixed up now and save yourself a second trip?" I went and got a nipple for the second bottle and filled the bottle with milk. With that done I came back upstairs and started to feed the deer. When he was done I said just a minute and went over to heat up the second bottle. The little deer just watched every move I made. She was ready to eat again when I brought the second bottle over to the place where I had given her the first bottle. Soon she was done and got herself into position to go out side. I said that was OK and out the door she and the rabbit went.

I could see through the window that they were out on the lawn eating away at the green grass like it was going out of style. Just munching away for all they were worth. I got busy with the dishes and got them all cleaned up for Grandma to see on her visit tomorrow. By the time I had finished the dishes it was almost two o'clock, so I got the 22 and started out for John Arco's place to go up to see all the kids that I'm sure their mom, or whoever she was, had told them about me coming to the place and I'd probably be back this afternoon. By the time I got up to John Arco's place, it must have been around three o'clock. That was ok and I just kept on going to the place. As soon as I got close I could hear kids playing out side. I put the 22 up against a tree and kept on going. I went up to the edge of the woods and just stood there. Pretty soon one of the kids shouted something in the foreign language that I had heard them speaking in before, and they all stopped playing and turned around to see where I was. When they all saw me they turned toward me and just looked. I then stepped out of the woods so they could all see me a little bit better and said, "Hello."

There was no response at all, they just stood there looking and wondering who I was. I said, "I'm Joe" that broke a little ice and a couple of the older ones said something that I couldn't understand at all. But at least they were talking to me. I gingerly put another foot out of the trees a little more toward them. When some of them had gotten a good look they started to jabber away in that same old language that had me baffled.

Then the two older boys came over to me and said, "Come on up and play with us." I did. I went out of the woods completely and was talking to them about what they were playing. I could see that they didn't understand me very well. I pointed to the house and said, "Momma." that they definitely understood and one of the boys went over to the house and went in for a minute or two. Soon he was back out again and had the woman in tow. She said, "Hello." Then she started to speak to them in their language.

This was all purely not understandable to me, so I just waited for her to finish what she was saying in another minute or so. Then she started in again in English, slowly so that they could understand her. She spoke very good English for a foreigner I thought. When she finished the little talk the kids all gathered around me and said where was my dog and where was my other pets. Seems like their "momma" had told them about the little deer, though I don't know how she knew about it at all. She just smiled at me and didn't say another thing.

It seems that they had been playing a sort of tag game when I had come out of the woods. They went right back to it after their mom had spoken and they invited me into the game too. But I didn't know the object of the game or the rules of play, so I just sat down on the sidelines and watched, hoping that something would become apparent soon.

Time just seemed to whiz on by and soon it started to get dark outside. I said that I had to get back to the farm. The kids all gathered around me and said that it was nice of me to come, and would I come again soon. I said sure I would, if they really wanted me to come. They all came over to the woods and wanted to know where the farm was. I pointed almost straight West and said about a mile or so.

I then told them to walk down the railroad track until they got to the bridge and to turn south right at the bridge. I told them that they could come tomorrow if they wanted to, when my grandmother would be there. They said that maybe they would come tomorrow. With that I took off through the woods again to get back to the farm. On the way I saw a couple of more crows and, I plinked off a shot and thought that I had missed them both. As I got up near where the crows had been sitting on a branch there was one of them lying down on the ground deader than dead. I picked it up and took it back to the farm with me.

Grandpa was wondering where I had been so I told him about all the kids up at the place on the other side of John Arcos' place. He was very interested and when I told him how their mom spoke two languages he thought that was pretty neat. When he asked me what the languages were I had to tell him that all I knew was that she spoke English and a foreign one.

He said that was nice but he had a lot to do on the new house. He had been working on the problem of how to get it get down on the foundation walls. I said, "Why don't you get four big jacks and lower it down that way?" He looked at me very sternly and said, "I don't see how that would work at all." I said, "You just get some plank to set the jacks on, get the jacks all positioned at the right places and tow the house over to above the foundation walls. Then all you have to do is raise the house enough to clear the wheels and then lower it down to the foundation." He said that I should be an engineer for sure.

That was good enough, but we still had to eat supper, so off he went to get supper ready. I went on up to the cage to see my two friends that were there, sure enough they were there and as usual they were hungry again. I said, "Come on", and I started down the hill for the little house. They were way out ahead of me loping down the hill getting over to the little house. They both waited there for me to bring them out some bran. This I did as soon as I got there and the two of them started right in on their suppers.

After their bran was done the rabbit went out into the yard to eat some grass but the deer hung around like she wanted something more to eat. It dawned on me that maybe she was looking for a little more milk. Down the basement I went to get her a couple of bottles of milk and took them upstairs to get them heated up. In a short time the bottles were ready and I called her over to the chair and fed them to her. She drank the two bottles down like there wasn't going to be a tomorrow at all.

Then it was Grandpa's and my turn to put on the feedbag. When we were finished, I began to do the dishes and Grandpa sat down to read the Italian paper. When I had finished the dishes I went outside to be with my two friends and they were real glad to see me again. I stayed and played with them for a while. We stayed there in the yard until about nine o'clock and then I said for them to go back up to their cage, tomorrow promised to be a full day too. Without any further to dos I went in to go to bed. I got my clothes off and into the bed and practically before my head hit the pillow I was asleep.

The next morning I woke with a gnawing thought running around in my head. How had the woman known about the deer? It beat me how she had known, but she knew somehow. It just kept gnawing at me the whole morning. I had to go over to the chicken coop to fix up the birds and collect the eggs. While I was in the little house washing up the eggs I came to the conclusion that she must have relatives in town that knew about the deer. They would have told her I'm sure, but just who they were was a mystery to me. Maybe one of Aunt Ada's customers who had been talking to Aunt Ada knew the mom of the parcel of kids and had told her about the deer.

It wouldn't matter much in the long run I kept thinking to myself. About noon the other car came into the farm, and there was aunt Dora and Grandma. Grandma was all words and talking away a mile a minute. Grandma wanted to know if I had taken good care of her chickens. I just said for her to go and look for herself, and she said she would do that for sure. She was most happy about all the eggs that were ready for the store and she was particularly happy about them all being cleaned and put in cartons. There must have been about twelve dozen eggs ready for the store. Grandpa said that I had done all the work on the eggs. Then he told her about my finding the hole in the wall and how much I had helped him put the new cement up on the coop.

She was just amazed at all the work that I had done. Grandpa also told her about the two fish that I had caught, and that I thought she should take them into town to the store to sell them. She was real happy about that. Then she went out to go over to the chicken coop to see for herself what Grandpa and I had done to the coop. She had picked up another dozen or so eggs and brought them into house to be cleaned. I got the fresh water from the creek and started right in cleaning them. The job took about a half hour.

She sat and watched me the whole time, talking all the while. When I had gotten the job done and put the eggs into a cartons she wanted to know if I would like to have a job. I said no, because school would be starting soon and I'd have to be in town for that, but thanks anyway. "That's too bad." She said. Then she said, "But you could work on Saturdays and Sundays couldn't you?" I said that I would have to ask my mother and father if it would be all right. In the mean time I was there for another week or two. She thought that was all right. Since she hadn't paid me for the work up until now, I didn't figure to collect any money for the time in the two weeks ahead.

Aunt Dora got the car loaded and then started to leave. She asked, "Would you like to go to town with me?" I said, "No thanks." Off she went across the field, up the trace and out of sight. We didn't see her again until the next afternoon when it was time to pick up Grandma, but then only for a minute. Grandma was eager to go. Without delay, she got into the car, shut the door and said to Aunt Dora, "Lets go child." Then off they went, headed into the sunset for town.

It was just as well that they didn't waste any time leaving because I still had the deer and the rabbit to take care of, so up the hill I went to get to the cage. There were the two of them waiting for me. When they saw me coming up the hill they came out of the cage and came down the hill to meet me. Surprise. Surprise. What a wonderful surprise that was.

I just turned around and started down the hill again. They were right behind me all the way down to the little house. When I went into the basement to get the two bottles of milk that I had fixed up that morning the little deer came long with me and when she saw the milk bottles she turned around and went back up the stairs. She went all the way to the upstairs over by the stove and stood waiting for me to get there. I got out the pan to heat the milk bottles in. Then I had to reach down to the wood box for wood to put in the stove and a piece of paper to burn to set the wood on fire.

All this took a few minutes, but the deer just stood there and watched me the whole time as if she was memorizing the routine to get it down pat for the next time. When a few minutes had gone by I took one of the bottles out of the pan of water and tested the milk for temperature and it was still a little cool, so I put it back in the pan again to let it get a little warmer. Then I tested it again and turned around to feed the deer.

She was all set to drink the milk down and went to it like there was no tomorrow. As she finished the first bottle she made a little sound and looked up at me as to say, "Where is the other bottle, please?" I was just getting the second bottle out for her and she was very anxious to get at it. She took the bottle and started swigging away at it for all she was worth. Pretty quick she was done and then she just stood there for a few more minutes looking at me with those big beautiful eyes, then turned for the door and went outside to munch on grass.

There was Spike and the rabbit looking at each other eye to eye, so to speak. They didn't even turn around when I came outside. They just stood there like they were carrying on a conversation. This lasted about twenty minutes and they finally quit the staring at each other and went on to more meaningful things, like eating grass and such. Spike left the area and the rabbit and the deer soon started for the cage, maybe to take a nap. I also was ready for a nap and went into the house to do so. Then Grandpa came in right behind me and said that he was going to take a nap. He lay down on the bed and promptly went to sleep, which only left me in a standing position. I said, "to bed" and crawled into the sack and also went to sleep.

It must have been at least seven o'clock when I woke up, and there was Grandpa standing by the stove cooking our supper. He saw me getting up and said, "You're just in time for supper." I finished getting up and then got the plates and silverware out and put them on the table. When he had everything ready, Grandpa said let's eat and so we did just that. When supper was done we went outside to sit in the cool of the evening.

Then Grandpa said, "Why don't you go fishing?" I went in and got my fishing rod and went down to the island. I cast the lure out about to the end of the pond and began reeling in slowly. No bites at all. I cast out again only this time I cast the lure over on the far side of the pond and started to reel it in. Then suddenly there was like an explosion in the pond just where my lure was. It was another fish and it felt at least as heavy as the other two fish.

I reeled in the line as carefully as I could, until I had the fish right up to the island. Then I took him by the line and put him up on the mainland. He sure looked as big or bigger than the other two fish. I left the lure in his mouth and carried him by the line over to where Grandpa was sitting to show him the fish. He said that looks like a nice sized fish. What do you think it weighs? I said at least ten pounds. Then I took the hook out of its mouth and Grandpa took it over to the scale to weigh it. He set it down on the scale and said that it weighed in at a full fifteen pounds.

The fish was as long as I was tall to say the least. With that Grandpa got out the waxed paper and knife and went to work cleaning the fish. Then Grandpa said that we had to keep the fish for Grandma to sell in the store. I said, "OK, Grandpa." and then went out to put the rod and reel away. I was pretty happy and went up to the cage to see my friends. They were both sound asleep on the hay they chose for their bed so I didn't disturb them at all. I just went down to the little house to go to sleep.

Thursday, there was nothing much doing except for the chickens that I had to take care of. That was the only duty that I could remember except that I went over to the chicken coop, got some feed out for the birds, fixed up their nests with new hay and then got the basket and began picking up the eggs. This task took me a little while longer because all the birds were back in their nests by then. I gently moved the birds off their perches in the nests and got the many eggs that were there. I went over to the door and got ready to take all of the eggs over to the little house when I heard some talking from the outside. What in the world was that all about? I asked myself.

I couldn't figure out what the heck was going on. I stepped outside and saw the last of a group of kids going across the bridge headed over toward the little house. I quickly got out of the chicken coop and ran over to the bridge. Some of the kids saw me running and stopped the rest of them to wait for me. I got over there and found that these were all of the boys and girls from the place up the other side of John Arco's place. I couldn't imagine what they were all doing here at the farm. One of the boys said, "We would love to see the deer and the rabbit". I said, "Just a minute" so that I could take the basket of eggs over to the little house. As I was coming back, I looked up the hill toward the cage.

Here were the rabbit and the deer coming somewhat timidly down the hill. I went over to meet them. I tried to tell them about the visitors that we had, but they didn't seem to understand at all. I turned around and started to go down the hill. Just then the kids spotted us coming down and they let out a scream that could be heard all the way in town! The deer and the rabbit spun around and ran back up the hill to the cage.

That was enough for me. I went over to the bunch of kids, for that was all they were was "a bunch of kids"! I got a little hot under the collar, I guess, and I told them all in no uncertain terms that they had messed up their own plans to see my two friends, and they said OK.

After I recovered from being angry, I told the kids to wait there in the hot sun and I would go see what I could do. I went up to the cage and tried to get the deer and the rabbit calmed down a little bit. I had a hard time just getting the two of them to accept me. Soon they came around and they decided that at least I wasn't to blame for the kids making all that noise. They both came over to me and let me pet them. It wasn't long before the little deer lifted her head up to mine and gave me a big wet kiss. I thought, for sure, things were going to be all right. After a few more minutes of petting them I started to go out of the cage and they followed me right away.

I led them down the hill to the yard where the kids all were waiting. You should have seen the faces on the kids, they were all smiles from ear to ear, and radiant, I'd say. I told them to just look. Then one of the older boys said it would be nice if they could come over to pet the two animals nicely. I said it would be OK but it would have to be one at a time. With that they all started jabbering away, but quietly and got in a line to come and pet the deer and the rabbit. It's funny how they lined up. The older boys came first followed by the younger boys. They were followed by the older girls and then came the younger girls. I didn't tell them how long to pet the animals but each one took about a minute or so. After doing the petting routine they formed a group over in the shade by the little house.

It was about time for the deer and the rabbit to eat, so I said lets all go over to the little house and the kids followed me and my two friends to the little house. I said for them to wait in the yard while I went down and got two bottles of milk. When I came up, the children were as excited as can be. The deer was allowing them to pet it and the rabbit was staying close by. I went up stairs and started the little fire to heat up the milk. When it was warm I went outside to the audience and the little deer came right over to me to get her milk. The kids were all surprised to see her eat so much and so fast. They just stood and watched for the whole time. When the deer was done she just looked up at me as if to say, "Pass the next bottle please." I gave it to her right away. While she was drinking the second bottle, I told the kids to go up the hill by the cage and watch for her when she came up there. They all ran up the hill happy as a bunch of larks.

When she was done with the second bottle she wanted to lie down but I told her, "No." She looked at me very funny and then decided that she had better go on up to the cage. She turned and started to go up to the cage, but then she caught sight of all the kids up there and didn't want to go. I started to go up to the cage and almost immediately she thought that would be all right and came along. The rabbit, in the meanwhile, had wandered way down by the creek and didn't see us go up to the cage. It looked around and we were all gone. That must have been a little nerve racking for it, because it came running up from the creek and caught up to the deer and me about half way to the cage, then it followed us the rest of the way. When the kids saw us coming they all started to talk and at least held it down to a gentle roar, if there is such a thing. Then the deer and the rabbit both got a little scared and stopped in their tracks.

I spoke softly to them and when I had gained their confidence back, I went ahead to the gate of the cage. The two of them followed me into the cage and went immediately for the hay over in the corner. Both of them lay down but didn't go to sleep. They just lay with their heads up looking at the kids and the kids were standing around two sides of the cage looking at the deer and the rabbit. Pretty soon, Grandpa called me for lunch. So I said, "I'm sorry but its lunch time and we have to go. Thank you all for coming. Come again some time and bring your mom and dad with you." With that, we all left the deer and the rabbit in the cage and started down the hill again.

I told the kids to be real careful when they were on the tracks and to look in both directions for trains. With that, they took off on their way home. I was surprised that their mother hadn't come looking for them but I suppose that she knew the older kids were along and they would watch out for the younger kids.

Then I immediately went up to the cage to get the two and to bring them down to the yard to eat some more grass. They were both happy to see me back and came right away when I called them. I was a happy camper to say the least. The deer and the rabbit were down by the little house eating away in the grass. Grandpa wanted to know who all the kids were. So I said that they were from the place just beyond John Arcos' place. He was genuinely surprised and said so.

All during lunch we talked about them and tried to figure out just who they were. We didn't come to any real conclusions but we had a lot of ideas on who they were and where they came from. After lunch I cleaned up the dishes and put them away.

Then I got the 22 and went out to go hunting again. I went up the pasture hill to the woodchuck den and as I was coming to the place I didn't see a thing. During the last twenty yards or so I bent over in a crouch and went along real slow. Pretty soon I was behind a little bush and I stopped to get a good look at the mound and the holes. Sure enough there was a chuck in one hole sticking his head out and looking the other way. I cocked the 22, and sighted it, and pulled the trigger. After the shot I couldn't see any thing so I went up to the hole and took a look. There in the woodchuck hole lay the dead chuck with a small hole in his head, deader than dead, as they say in the old country. I was pretty happy, to say a thing or two. I just left the chuck where it was. I said to myself, "Let's go see if the chucks have come back to potato hill," and started off across the pasture.

Near the bottom of the hill comes Spike running like there was no tomorrow. Soon he caught up with me and after a few minutes of scratching his ears and him licking my face we were ready to start off again. Generally Spike was in quite a humorous mood after running up to the woodchucks mound and checking out the dead chuck and then he came back. Now all I had to do was to go over to potato hill to check on the chucks over there. The two of us meandered through the pasture. Before we got there I told Spike to be quiet and he settled down into his pointing mood, all nice and quiet but ears perked up and attentive.

Just as we came up to the potato patch he went into his pointing mode again, all quiet with one foot off the ground. He stayed that way for ten minutes or more and kept looking over at me as if to say, "there's a chuck out there dumbbell." I crept nearer to the potato patch to see for myself and sure enough there was a chuck out in the field, trying to dig out the potatoes. I took aim and shot the chuck. Spike went racing out to the potato patch where the chuck lay dead, grabbed the chuck in his mouth and shook it for all he was worth, finally stopping after five minutes or so. When I got up to him he was all smiles as if to say, "See what I caught." Then I picked the chuck up by the tail and walked up to the front of the field. When I got there I looked at the holes to see if the dead chucks were still there, and they were. Where had this, now dead, chuck come from anyhow? It was puzzling to say the least. I thought that after I had shot the other two chucks that the remaining chucks would have abandoned the den. I'd have to look into it some other day. Right now I had to go my two friends in the cage waiting for me.

With that I took off for the cage with Spike right behind me till the bottom of the hill and then he took off on his own. He just up and left me for the wolves to eat me I guess. Anyhow when I got up to the cage there he was playing footsie again with the deer and rabbit. I came up to the cage and the deer and rabbit both came over to me. The deer stood up on her hind legs with her front legs on my chest and reached over and licked my face. The rabbit just sat there and waited until we were done. When I bent over to talk to her for a little while, she surprised me like I had never been surprised before. She stretched out her hind legs; stood up on them and before I knew it she licked my face too. Boy what a day this was turning into! Wow!

I stayed and played with the two of them for about an hour and then went down to the little house. Grandpa was just making supper so I got cleaned up and set the table. We had a good supper and then I washed the dishes and went over to the chair to sit down. In a little while I decided to go to bed. I got undressed and crawled into the sack. Another day had passed and no turmoil was allowed to happen.

The Cherry School

Schooldays were almost upon us and I was wondering what to do about my two pets. I just couldn't leave them alone in the cage. I was concerned that maybe Grandpa wouldn't have time for them. I was really worried about them and what would happen to them if I weren't around when they really needed me. On Monday of the coming week I was scheduled to start school and then where would I be? I just couldn't leave them there without me to look after them. What if some day soon they were to wake up in the morning and they couldn't find me or wouldn't go to Grandpa? That would be a real tragedy. All they did in school was play games all day, and run around the play yard chasing each other. But Grandpa said that I had to go to school. It was the law that everybody had to have an education. What's an education for anyway?

I just put the thoughts aside for the moment and went on to other things. "Who needs an education anyway?" I thought. Education is for older kids that are playing baseball and football and are in active sports. Its not for us younger fellas not dry behind the ears yet. Besides, I'd rather be here on the farm than go to a school building and waste most of the day. What was all the fuss about? Who needed to go to school every day when I could be here on the farm having fun everyday? Maybe Grandpa would know. I'll ask him at suppertime when we have a little time to talk. The rest of the day I just hung around the little house and went up to play with my two friends, the deer and the rabbit.

When suppertime was there, I got out the plates and silverware and got all cleaned up to eat. We sat down and started eating. When we were almost done I asked Grandpa about school. He said that he was very much in favor of schools in general but especially for young people like myself. He went on to say that without schools we would be living in a country like a bunch of baboons, with no ideas about anything at all. He took me outside and showed me the railroad bridge and said that it took a good education to build it and the same goes for the railroad tracks. Also, it took an education to build the trains that ran on the railroad and the steam shovels that placed the iron ore into the cars in the train. He said that it took a good education for someone to build the trucks that my Dad used to go get the beer and deliver it around the range cities. He said that it took a good education to learn where the iron ore was and how to get it out of the ground. He said that it took a good education to make the blast furnaces that made the steel from the ores.

Then he said that I would be starting school on Monday morning at the school in the place called Cherry. He thought that some of the kids that had been here at the farm to see the deer and rabbit would also be going to school in Cherry. He said, "Think how nice that would be." I didn't see it that way, but I let him have his say about it. On Sunday afternoon we went for a ride in the sulky all the way down to Cherry school, to show me the way and where it was and all that. When we got back he said to mark the time down so I'd know just how long it took to go there. Then he said that tomorrow I could take the horse and sulky down to school and park the horse there in the schoolyard with the sulky and then I could come back to the farm.

Early the next morning we had breakfast and I was dressed up in a brand new outfit, new shoes, new pants, and new shirt and was ready to go at 7:00 AM. Then we had to get the harness on the horse and get the sulky out of its place. By then it was 7:30AM and I figured that I had better leave. Off I went in the sulky with the horse pulling for all she was worth. I soon got to school and then tied the horse up to the tree in the schoolyard. I figured that I must be late because there were no kids around at all.

Soon a woman drove in and parked her car next to the sulky. She got out of the car and came over to me. She looked me over, had me turn around and then started to talk in that foreign language. When she stopped I said in English, "I don't understand the language at all." Her jaw dropped down about a foot and she hemmed and hawed trying to say something but just couldn't make the words come out. Until finally she did say, "What do you mean you don't understand the language?" I said, "What language is it?" she says, "Its Finnish of course!" I said, "I'm an Italian boy." She was pretty shook up about that little bit of news to say the least.

She was still reeling mentally and said, "Are you coming to school here?" I said, "Of course I am! Else why would I be here?" That last one really got to her and she hit her forehead with palm of her hand. Then she said, "I don't think you had better try that out, because this is an all Finish language school and nobody here speaks Italian. They all speak Finnish, and some speak only the Finnish language." I said, "That leaves me out then, I guess." She said, "Yes, I guess it does. But what will you do?" I replied, "I would go to school in Hibbing where there are some civilized people." That little statement coming from a five year old was just about the limit of her endurance. She took off for the school building in a huff saying that she couldn't teach all of the others to speak English in just an hour to say nothing about the next few years. I left it there and untied the horse from the tree where she was standing with a forlorn look about her, just wondering what all the words were about, anyhow.

With that out of the way, I got up into the sulky and began driving back to the farm. I hadn't gone more than a half-mile when I came upon all my new friends from the place up behind John Arco's place. They all waved and wanted to know how the little deer was today. When I told them that she seemed all right when I left her, they were relieved indeed. Then they wanted to know why I was down this way. I said, "To go to school but the teacher said that she couldn't make Englishmen out of all her students in an hour. Here I am." They said that they could understand that part, but what was I going to do?" "I'm just going to have to go to school in Hibbing, I guess." I replied. They all said that they were sorry and couldn't understand that at all. After all, they could learn about English too. I replied, "That was OK with me. I'd just have to go to school in Hibbing and like it." With that they took off again on their way to school and I took off on my way back to the farm.

When I got there I just left the horse hooked up to the sulky and I went into the little house to sit down. There was Grandpa just sitting there in a chair, thinking. When he saw me he got all flustered and said, "Why aren't you in school like you should be?" He went on to rant and rave about how important school was to everybody especially to young boys! When he got settled down again I told him about what the teacher at the school had said about it being an all-Finnish school and how she couldn't be expected to teach all the students to speak English just to accommodate me. He said that that was understandable and he supposed that I could go to school in Hibbing, but that I would have to move into town. Now that was a real blow coming from my Grandpa! To bring it in the open was as harsh as I could stand it. I just had to be apart by myself for a little bit and ran outside and up to the cage where I knew that at least they weren't against me.

There they were, the two of them waiting for me. At least they were happy to see me, and both of them came over to me. I had never before experienced such love and devotion, I was just overwhelmed and it brought tears to my eyes. Never before had such a simple act of recognition meant so very much. I just sat down and cried, petting them both all the time. This went on for a couple of hours when the deer got up to her feet and walked over to the door, then she turned around and looked at me with those two big, beautiful eyes. Then it came to me that she was hungry and wanted me to get her some milk.

Down the hill I went and into the basement. I got two bottles of milk and took them upstairs to heat them up.

The two of them were eager as can be to get to the milk. But wait a minute. Why was the rabbit so anxious to get the milk? Could it be that she too was a milk drinker? The only thing I could do was to get another bottle and test her. Down the basement I ran to do just that and when I had the bottle full I fixed it up with a nipple and I took it upstairs to heat it up a little. The deer had spent all this time patiently waiting for me to get done and then waited for a few more minutes for me to heat up the bottle. Then I held the two bottles out for them to start eating and was surprised at the little rabbit. She took to her bottle like it was going out of style, as did the little deer. When the deer got the first bottle done I gave her the second one. When they were both done with their lunch I said for them to wait out in the yard while Grandpa and I had our lunch.

With them outside I set the table for Grandpa and me, and then I sat down to wait for Grandpa to come in. In a few more minutes he came in and said it's time for lunch and proceeded to fix it up and onto the table. After we had eaten I got up to do the dishes. Then I told Grandpa about the rabbit eating milk with the deer. He was just taken aback with news about the rabbit eating milk, and from a bottle at that. He couldn't believe me at all. I showed him the three bottles and said that I didn't believe it either. He said at first that it had to be a first in the animal kingdom. He went out the door scratching his head and mumbling to himself. I guess it was kind of hard to believe at that.

The very next day who should show up at the farm but my Mom and Dad? My Mother was all in an uproar about me trying to go to school in Cherry yesterday. I couldn't believe it at all. Here was my quiet little mother being louder than ever, ranting and raving about my going to a Finlander's school in a Finnish area. Why a good little Italian boy would even think of doing such a thing was beyond comprehension. She was just about ready to fire the first shot and start a war over it. That, too, was beyond me, just as the teacher at the school was beyond me. It didn't make a lot of sense to me at the time, and I said so. That little discussion was way over my head to start with, so I just stayed out of the conversation. Pretty soon my Mother said for me to get all my things together because she was taking me to town right now! I went over to my Grandpa and asked him if he would feed my two friends every day. When he said that he would, I was most happy and gathered up my things. I said, "I'm ready. Let's go." Then I ran out to the car and got in it. Soon my Mom and Dad came out. They also said goodbye to my Grandpa, got in the car, and we were off for town.

We had to go to town by way of Dupont Lake because the men were still working on the bridge at Mohkas' place. Seems like it was taking a year or so to get the bridges done. It only seemed that way because they had been at it for more than a month already. If they needed the time, they needed the time, and that's all there was to it. If it took them a year, then we would have go on Dupont Road for a year. When we got into town my Dad said, "Why the heck were you trying to go to the Cherry school?" I said, "Because Grandpa had sent me there." That seemed to have ended the argument about the school.

We weren't heading to the store today. We were heading to the popshop where they had been finishing the new rooms in the apartment. Mother said to go to my room. It was only the first time that I was in the apartment area above the popshop and I didn't know quite how to get there, so I said, "Where is my room?" The two of them looked at me like I was pulling their legs, and they said, "Right over there on the right." Over there on the right I went and found the room right a way. With that done I got ready for bed and my Mother came and said, "You've got to take a bath before you get in bed, so come on out here." I immediately came out to the kitchen and she motioned to the bathroom. In I went to take a bath, something different from the farm where we bathed in the creek. When I was done my mother came into the bathroom and washed up my back. Then got me out of the bathtub and dried me all over. Real nice service if you ask me.

The next morning my Dad gave me a ride up to the Washington School and took me in to the Kindergarten room and introduced me to the teacher, Miss Curry. She was a very nice lady and seemed to know my Dad quite well, and incidentally, she sang at my wedding in later years. That much had gotten me into the school building and into class, but I still had to explain why I was a day late getting there. When my Dad had left, I proceeded to tell her why I was a whole day late for the start of school. Then she said that she didn't believe it at all. I told her to call the teacher at the Cherry school and ask her about the little kid with the horse and sulky that was there on Monday. She did, called the teacher up long distance to ask her about the little boy and the horse and sulky that was there yesterday morning. When she came back into the room she said that teacher wanted to know how she knew about it. "Oh," she said, "He's here in my room now to begin school today." That's how I got to finally be in school and started enjoying it.

So much for the niceties, but I was wondering how my two little friends were doing on the farm. I couldn't help wondering all day and all that week too. They didn't teach me very much in school that week. Only playing around and getting used to taking orders. When the weekend came I was all ready to go to the farm. My Mom said, "No farm today and that's that!" As much as I tried to tell her about my two friends and how they would miss my not being at the farm, she just wouldn't listen to me at all. I was crestfallen. I didn't know what to do. I just walked around the popshop building for the whole day. On Saturday night after I was in bed I got to thinking about the farm road and how to get to it.

I was thinking about walking to the farm if I could just remember what the route was. I thought and thought about it for almost the whole night. When morning came I had the answer all arranged in my head.

It was Sunday morning and I had to go to Church with Mom and Dad. Right after Church there was breakfast to eat. I got that out of the way. I went to my room to change clothes and to get some of my things together to take with me. Then out the door I went and over to the Brooklyn road, and started walking down the road toward the highway. Dick Bartol, who was in the beer business like my dad, waved to me and said hello. I waved back to him and mumbled hello and kept on going right down the hill and on to 13th Street on my way. I thought that I shouldn't go all the way on 16th Avenue because the family of my mothers' cousin lived there and would call my mother for sure. I turned south on 16th Street and went down it to get over to Argir Street to get to 12th Street.

When I got to 12th Street it looked as if I was going to make it all the way, so off I went on the way to the farm. Just then I looked up and saw my father driving on 15th Street. I got scared so I ducked in between the houses to hide for a while. I stayed there for about five minutes or so and then came out from between the buildings and started walking again. I was very careful then to watch for my Dad driving by. If he had seen me it would be the end of my little trip. Things went along fairly well for the next five blocks or so and then I was at the Highway. Only a short walk of about two miles and I would be on the road to the farm. That seemed to only take a few minutes and there was the road. I just took off on the road at the Rocklawn Dairy and kept on going at a good clip.

I was making good time and it seemed like in no time at all I was getting close to Mohkas place. Then I was wondering if the bridge was completed yet. All I could do was keep on walking to the hills by the river. When I got there I found that they hadn't finished the bridge yet and I'd have to find another way across. I went ahead down to the river looking for a place to cross. Lucky for me the men had left a footbridge in place so I crossed the river on it and went up the hill on the other side of the river. I thought that that was just like being down town, it was so easy. Now I only had about four more miles to go to make it all the way to the farm. When I got to the highway I looked very carefully in both directions and then took off on the trace over which the new house had come.

Man this was like eating candy at the ice cream store! The eight or ten miles had gone off like a charm and I wasn't even tired after all my walking. I kept going until I got to the township road that ran behind the farm and over the railroad tracks. I thought "It's only about another mile or less to the farm buildings." I started on the trace down the hill to the corner of the field through which the house had been towed. I climbed over the gate there and started to walk across the field. When I looked up there was Grandpa standing on the hill above the haunted woods. I shouted and waved my arms to him, he just stood there taking his hat off, scratching his head, and waited for me.

This was just like old home week. I ran up to him and hugged him around the legs. When I let up on the hugging he said, "Have you seen your deer and the rabbit?" I understood right away what he meant by the seriousness of the question that the two of them were gone. I said, "No I haven't Grandpa. How long have they been gone?" He said, "I don't know for sure but I think that they had walked off about two o'clock or so, because I fed them just about 1:30." I said, "Don't worry. They'll show up when they get hungry." With that we turned and went toward the house. He then asked if my Dad was coming down to pick me up, and I said he probably would when they figured out that I was here.

But all that had left me concerned about my two friends. I didn't know what I should do at all. I was worried sick. Where could they be? Were they all right? Maybe I should have stayed at home so that I would not have known about them being gone until some time tomorrow afternoon. I was really worried about them now. I told my Grandpa that. He said not to worry, that they were probably all right.

I couldn't do the "not worry" thing. They were my friends, the only real friends that I had left in the world since Ronny had gone to Arizona with his mother and my sister Patsy. I said for Grandpa to call Spike up here. He did when we were on our way back to the cage.

When we got there good old Spike was there waiting for us in his usual happy state, jumping around and barking. I said, "Spike do you know where they are?" He just looked around the cage and back to me as if to say he didn't know where they had gotten to either.

To get a good smell of the deer and the rabbit, I took him to the corner where all the hay was laying around and I said, "Go find them for me, please Spike." He took right off looking for them. He went out the way we had come into the cage and went down to the Haunted Woods right off. Pretty soon he came out of the woods and ran along the edge of the woods going north. When he got to the top of the Grain Shed hill, he kind of stopped and looked for quite a while toward the pasture beyond the hill. I guess that was supposed to mean that they were gone for sure.

Pretty soon he came back to the cage kind of down in the dumps with his head held down and tail not wagging as it usually was. Seems like he knew the two of them were gone for sure. I just couldn't take that and started to cry a little. Grandpa said I was not to worry and that they would show up in the morning. With that he said that we should go back to the house. He wanted to talk to my Dad about something when he came down to the farm to get me. We went down to the little house to wait for dad. We only had to wait for an hour or so, maybe not even that much time. Grandpa said, "Here they are now." and went outside to meet them. My mother came running into the house all flustered. She began to raise a little heck about my walking all the way down to the farm, especially without telling them about my going. I could tell that she was relieved though to find me here at the farm.

I told her about my two friends that were gone. She listened to what I had to say and then she said that I was not to worry about them, that they would be back as soon as they got good and hungry. I said, "I sure hope so." With that we went outside to where Grandpa and my dad were. They were up on the hill where the new house was going to be set down, talking away a blue streak. They then came down to where we were still talking away a mile a minute. My Dad was saying that he thought that he could get necessary heavy-duty jacks and he would bring them down in the big beer truck, on Friday. Grandpa said that would be fine and that he would have everything ready by then.

My dad said that we had better go. My mother said Ok, and started to get in the car, but she stopped and told me to get in first, so I did. We started the car and turned it around to face the outgoing track across the field. Soon we were on our way to town again. Neither of them said a word about my walking away that day. They were as quiet as two non-conversant church mice.

They didn't say a word until we were home and upstairs. Then they both let loose on me at once. "What did you mean by walking down to the farm? Why didn't you tell us about being unhappy? Why didn't you do this or why didn't you do that?" Seems like they just went on for hours until I went into my room and closed the door. I just lay there in bed, not sleeping, thinking about where my two little friends could be. My mother came in about 11:00 o'clock and said, "Aren't you sleeping yet? Now turnover and get to sleep." I turned over but I didn't go to sleep, at least not right away. It took me about two more hours, just lying there, before I got to sleep.

When morning finally came I got dressed for school and went out to the kitchen to eat my breakfast. As soon as breakfast was done, I was off to Washington School. It was a long walk. It must have been about fourteen or fifteen blocks, at least. I walked as fast as my legs would carry me. I got there in plenty of time and just sat down in the playground thinking about the two animals out at the farm. I was wondering just where they were and how they were getting along. When the bell rang for class I got up and went into the building, but it wasn't with a lot of smiling happiness. Darn it, I was still worried about my pets. Miss Curry said, "What's the matter, Joey?" Then I told her about my two pets and pretty soon all the other kids had stopped what they were doing and were standing around Miss Curry and I, listening in.

They all wanted to know how I ever got a deer and a rabbit as pets. Miss Curry said, "Go ahead and tell them but I want you to come up here to the front of the room." She got all the other kids to sit down and then said for me to tell all of them about the little deer and the rabbit that I had out on the farm. I felt pretty strange up there, in front of everybody, but I told them that I had a deer and a rabbit for friends. I told them how I had gotten them. I told them about how Spike had brought in the rabbit. I told them how both the deer and the rabbit had come to me for their food each day. I told them all about my fixing up three bottles of milk each day; how the two of them would come to me and eat the bran and milk I had fixed for them. I told them how good it made me feel. I also told them how lonely it was without them and how much I missed them.

By this time it was getting close to 11:00 o'clock and Miss Curry said that I should take my seat. In going back to my seat I saw all the other teachers and the school principal who had come in to the room to listen in on my story. When the principal went to leave, he said, "I just want to say that I know this story is all true because I saw little Joey with the deer here in town one day this summer. I know that Joey would not make up such a story." I said, "No I wouldn't make up such a story. They are both gone now that I've come into town to go to school." That made many of the kids sad, as well as Miss Curry. The principal said that we could have the rest of the morning off. Miss Curry said that she would be out on the playground if any of wanted to stay around the school, which I thought was very nice of her. We all got a little vacation from school that day.

I went along home and when I got there my Dad said, "Go up and eat your dinner because we are going to the farm, and hurry up, too." I went up stairs and told my Mom about going to the farm. She fed me and I changed my clothes to be presentable to the animals and out the door, and down the stairs I went flying all the way. When I got downstairs my Dad said that we were going in the truck today. I jumped up into the cab of the truck and was ready to go. My Dad said that we had to make a little stop at the mining company lot on Lincoln Street and then we would be already to go. When we got to Lincoln Street and turned at the mining company yard the gate guard wanted know what we wanted and my Dad said, "We're here to get a couple of jacks for Mr. Catterini." The gate guard said that we were supposed to pick them up at the round house, and gave us the instructions on how to get there.

We drove in the yard to the South entrance gate and then turned right to get to the round house. When we got there we found the mining boss was there to welcome us, and he had a whole crew of men there waiting for us. He said that the jacks were kind of heavy and he didn't know if our "Little Truck" could carry the load or not. My Dad said that the truck was licensed up to 70,000 lbs of weight. Then the boss said, "That's not enough, the load will be about 85,000 pounds or so. You'd better let me get a mining company truck to take the jacks." My Dad said OK. The superintendent said for one of the men to get a truck to haul the jacks to the farm. When he came back he was in a great big truck, a dump truck that stood about 16 feet tall and maybe 30 feet long. He backed the truck into the loading dock and jumped out. The superintendent said for him to get the jacks loaded and then to follow Dad's beer truck to wherever he was going.

This he did with a big smile on his face, singing all the time, while the rest of the guys looked at him with eyes full of want themselves. When the loading of the jacks was done he said, "I suppose I'd better take two or three of you guys along to help me get them unloaded too." With that there was a heck of a noise from all the men who wanted to be in the unloading crew. The truck driver was a big man so he picked two of the biggest men in the crew and said, "Let's go." The three of them got into the big truck and said, "Let's get moving." to my Dad. Dad said for me to get in the beer truck, he got in the other side of the truck and started off for the farm.

When we got out to Lincoln Street he stopped the truck and got out for a minute. He went back to the big truck and talked to the man for a little bit, and then came back to the beer truck and said that I was supposed to get out of the truck and go back to the other truck. Out of the beer truck I jumped. One of the guys came from the mining truck and took my seat in my Dad's truck. Then we were off to the farm. What a ride I was having! Man Oh Man! I stood up on the seat while the big guy next to me put his arm around me so that I wouldn't fall out.

We rode along with me shouting "Hi" to all my friends on the way. We went down the Brooklyn Road and out to the Highway. The man driving the truck started to drive on the shoulder of the Highway and I asked him why. Then he told me that mining company trucks as big as this one weren't legal driving on State Highways. I asked what would the truck do to the tarve road that was up ahead. The big guy told me that we'd probably break it up, and we should find another road. I told him that we would only be on gravel roads all the way to the farm if we went through Kittsville and out the other side. He said, "That is a great idea but how do I get there?" I told him to take the very next left turn to get to Kitsville. He did that and there we were riding down the streets of Kitsville with me saying hi to all the kids.

Then out and across the Highway again and we were on the Kitsville Road. It was all gravel and the big man said that now we were all right. I said we sure were as long as I could remember the correct way to get to the farm. But I knew I could remember when I finally saw the Cutoff Highway up ahead. I told the guy to go straight across the Highway when he got to it. He said, "You sure know your way around these roads." I said, "I should, riding in the front seat with my Grandpa all the time." That road was narrow enough so that the mining company truck took the whole road, and the ditches on either side were deep with no shoulder room at all. The big guy driving the truck began to get a little worried. The culverts on any roadways into the fields were only made of sheet metal and probably wouldn't hold the truck. "What do we do if we meet another car?" he asked. "I guess they will have to back up to the next field road and let us by." I said. Sure enough that's what happened at the hill past Six Mile Lake and wouldn't you know it, the other driver was mad as all get out at us for taking up all the road. He refused to back up to the intersection where we had to turn right to get to the farm. Then our driver got out of the big truck and walked over to his driver's window and asked the guy to get out of his car and they would try to discuss this in an orderly manner. When the guy saw just how big our driver was he just put his car in gear and backed up the quarter mile or less to the intersection and turned into it. There he waited until we went by turning the other way to get to the farm.

I learned a very important lesson that day, that's for sure. Always take a big friend along with you in case of arguments. Anyway, we were on the last leg of the road to the farm, so I thought that I should be honest with the driver and tell him that we were all out of roads, so I told him exactly that. He said, "What do you mean that we are on the last drivable road?' I said, "Just wait a minute and you'll see what I mean." I told him to stop when we got to the top of the trace that went down to the farm. He wanted to know why. He said, that he'd better go look at that for sure and got down from the truck to go see for himself. When he got back, he wanted to know if the farm had a road into it or not. I said that it didn't have a road yet but that Grandpa was going to have to build a new road. The only road was the gravel that grandpa had put down for the house to go over.

"Oh," he said, "That sounds like it's just about up to par." He followed the trace down the hill. When he got to the gate at the bottom of the hill he said, "What do you think? Do you think I'll be all right driving in there on that gravel or not?" I said, "That's a good question. Remember why you are here. Those jacks in the back end are a little heavy to tug around very far."

With that, the big guy put it in gear and started driving on to the farm. He wanted to know, "Where do I go from here with the heavy load in the mining truck?" I said, "Go along the gravel road to the top of the first hill and turn left." He did so very nicely. When we got up to the top of the hill he could see the house sitting on the wheels and he wanted to pull into that area but I said to let me out first and I would go see about my two friends. Then I got out of the truck and ran up to the cage, but my two friends were not in the cage. I signaled the big guy to drive right on in. He came almost up to the new house and stopped. By then my Dad and Grandpa came up to the top of the hill. My Dad wanted to know which road we had come on. Then I told him that we came across on the Kitsville road and we met another driver that thought we should turn around and let him pass us and how the driver of the car had backed up when he saw just how big our driver was.

My Grandpa said that he had coffee on the stove for the big guy and his helpers. They should come down and have some, while we figured out how to unload and to reload the jacks. Down they came to the little house for their coffee. Much to my surprise the big guy wanted to know just exactly what the jacks were for. Grandpa told him that it was my idea to jack up the house, take the wheels out from under it and to set it down on the foundation walls. That was all well and good. But how were we going to put the jacks back in the mining company truck? Grandpa said, "Oh, that's the easy part." Then he proceeded to tell the Big Guy that that is where his team came into the picture, and if the three guys could stick around tomorrow he'd be happy to show them. "Oh," said the big guy, "We've got to get the truck back tonight but if it's ok we'll come down tomorrow and see you do it. Then my Grandpa said, "But when will you get the jacks back to the mining company? The Big Guy said, "Next week should be time enough for that." They all kind of laughed at that a little. When they had finished their coffee the big guy said, "Let's go, Walt" to my Dad and off they went leaving me behind at the farm. Don't get me wrong; I thought that it was a good idea.

After they left my Grandpa said to come up to the new house. The two of us went up to the new house. I didn't know why we came up here, but I was happy indeed for coming. There were my two friends, the deer and the rabbit. I was so glad to see them; I started to cry a little. I said, "Grandpa can I go feed them, please?" He said, "Yes you can." I took off like a banshee running all the way down to the little house, then into the basement to get the three bottles of milk. I raced up stairs to heat them on the stove and when they were ready so were my two friends. They came over to me and started to eat. They ate like there's no tomorrow. Gosh but it was good to have them back. I couldn't help but wonder where they had been. When they had finished eating I went outside again and up to the new house with the two of them following me all the way. They went into the cage and they both lay down to sleep. I went back over to where Grandpa was at the new house. He said right out that he didn't know the two of them were back, but he had a feeling all day about the two scallywags and they would be back sometime over the weekend. I told him that I was so glad that they were back.

Grandpa wanted to know where to put the four jacks. He was just kidding me along, when I said that he would have to put them on planks of wood. Good, heavy planks would be the things to have at each corner. Then he said to come along with him to see something else. I went with him down to the barn. There he opened up the door and there inside the barn were about ten or more heavy planks. I said, "Gosh Grandpa, where did you get these planks?" He said, "From your Dad, last Wednesday." Now all we had to do was to get them up to the new house, which he said he would do tomorrow morning after chores were done. He said that it was too bad that I wasn't a little taller so that I could hitch up the team for him. I looked long and hard at the team as I felt the same way. Maybe next year after I grow up a little, I'll be able to hitch up the team and take them outside.

The next morning was a real busy time. It started with Grandpa having breakfast ready at 5:30AM and when we were done eating we went over to the barn to get ready for the morning milking. I pumped the water in from the creek and then turned on the flow for the cows. They were very appreciative and let me know by their soft mooing. Grandpa got started with the milking and in about an hour or so he was done. Then we were ready for the whole day, which sat there in front of us. Up to the new house we went, got all the way up there and remembered that we needed the team and the planking. Back down to the barn we went. It took a little effort to get the team all harnessed up and ready to go. Soon we were back outside the front door of the barn with the team waiting to get attached to the planks. Grandpa had even remembered to get a chain to tow the planks with. He finally got them hooked up and said, "Let's go!" and started off across the barnyard toward the new house.

We had no more than started and in came a car. "Now who the heck is that!" said Grandpa, just as the big guy that was driving the mining company truck yesterday got out of it. Then the other two guys got out of the car. One of the men said, "Looks like we got here just in time!" Grandpa said very apologetically, "I don't even have coffee ready for you." The big guy said, "That's OK! Just tell me where these planks go." Grandpa said, "Just follow me." Then he proceeded to drive the team pulling the planks up the hill. When he got to the top of the hill and had turned left to get into the house area he said, "Right here" and stopped the team. All the men were eager and went over to get a plank to tow it to one corner of the lot. Then they came right back to get another of the planks to take. This went on for another half an hour, and the planks all had been delivered to their respective spots. Then Grandpa said it was time for coffee and went down the hill to make some.

The three guys and I came down the hill right after Grandpa. I hadn't seen my two friends, and I was wondering if they were in the cage or not. I went back up the hill and looked in the cage. There they were huddled together like they were scared or something. When they saw that it was me they came right over to me. I said, "I suppose your hungry." Then I started down the hill, but they were reluctant about coming with me. I went back to the cage and talked very gently to them both for a few minutes. This time they were ok to go. I started out of the cage and down the hill. Then I called out to the men saying that I had deer and a rabbit coming with me, and to hold the loud talking until I could get them fed. They replied, "OK!"

The deer and rabbit both came with me to the basement to get the bottles. When we were ready to go upstairs the two of them seemed a little reluctant. I talked to them very quietly telling them that there was nothing to worry about and that I would be with them the whole way. Soon they seemed ready to come upstairs to drink their milk, and I led the way. When we got up stairs the men all let out a, "WHOOP!" and scared the daylights out of my two friends. They tried to get out the door but I was in the way and caught the two of them. I talked to them very quietly for about a half an hour. They were calmed down enough by then for me to go and warm up their milk. I told the guys that they would see a first in about two minutes and started to feed the deer. When it came her turn the rabbit stood up on her hind feet and reached out with her head to get the bottle of milk. I fed the two of them that way until the bottles were all empty. The guys were just amazed! They didn't know what to think. They said so and they also apologized for the loud whooping they had done. I took my two friends outside for a minute and the three guys came outside too. I said, "Go up to the cage" to my two friends, and away they went up to the cage.

All three of the guys said, "Lets get back to work." and walked up the hill to the new house. Grandpa was up there already waiting for them. Then he hitched the horses up to the wheels and said gidyup and the horses took up the slack, and pulled the house in over the foundation walls. When the house was exactly in the right position, he had them stop pulling on the wheels. The men all said that it looked about right where it was. Grandpa unhooked the team and took them over to the barn to get the harnesses off them and put them in their stalls. Then back he came to the new house ready to lower it down to its foundation walls. The three men were ready, one at each corner and Grandpa at the other corner. They all raised the jacks, by pumping them up to the bottom of the house.

With that done Grandpa took the wheels out from under the house and took them down to the yard level away from the house. Then Grandpa gave the word to lower the house down to the basement walls. Soon enough the house was on its foundation. The men all let out a shout and walked around it to inspect it a little and congratulating each other on a job well done. Grandpa said that they had to congratulate me because it was my idea. When they heard that they all said, "I don't believe it." Grandpa said that he spent some long hours just thinking about it, and that was the only solution that he could come up with. With that job over and done with Grandpa asked what they would all like for lunch.

The men all said that they would have to go home for lunch. Grandpa said that he had a couple of chicken cooking and for the men to please stay because he had no other way to pay them for their morning's work. Let's go inside he said to them and we'll have a small glass of vino to go with our meal too. That got their attention for sure and they all said, "All right. Let's go inside!" Into the house they all went while I took a minute to run up the hill to see my two friends. When I got up there, they were nowhere to be found. The cage was empty and they weren't lying around out in the yard anywhere. With that my heart just sank. I had a feeling that they were gone but I just kept on looking for them. I even called Spike up to see if he could find them, and he did the same as he did the first time I called him. He went down to the haunted woods and up to the top of the grain shed hill and then just stood there in his pose with his ears perked up on his head, staring off into the distance. I took this maneuver to mean that the two of them were gone; I hoped it wasn't for good.

I went down to get some lunch. The three guys were just sitting around and talking. They all wanted to know about the deer and the rabbit. I told them that they were gone again, and I didn't know where they were. They said that they would watch for them on the way home today. I said thanks a lot but that I didn't feel it would do any good. That ended another exciting week in my childhood.

Give Me a Butch

The month went fairly fast as did the end of the year. Christmas vacation was liked by one and all. I spent as much time as I could out on the farm and enjoyed the winter mostly from indoors because it was so darn cold out all the time. I always wondered about my two little pets, I wondered where they were now. I wondered about what they might be doing now that the snow had come and where they were spending the winter. Were they still here on the farm? Were they gone down South a little ways? Were they up North some distance? What were they doing about food? Did they miss me not being at the farm? I had a million questions about them and no answers at all. I wondered about them all the time.

One day while I was walking in the high pasture, I thought I caught just a glimpse of a deer off in the woods. But it was hard to tell if I really saw it or not. I went over to where I had seen the image that so quickly disappeared. Sure enough the tracks were still there in the snow. It had been a deer that I saw. It was obviously a big deer judging by the size of the jumps it made getting away from me, so I knew that hadn't been my little deer. I continued to walk around the pasture hoping that I would catch sight of her. There was a rabbit going under a bush and I ran up to the bush to see if she was my friend or not, but she took off running as soon as I got there so it couldn't have been my friend.

I turned and started for the little house watchful as ever ahead and to both sides, but without any luck at all. When I got to the pasture fence line I crossed over it and found that I was on top of potato hill and it wasn't a pasture fence line at all but a new line that Grandpa had put in during the fall. I continued to walk on toward the little house and couldn't help but wonder what do woodchucks do in the winter when the ground is all frozen? I wondered if they froze like the ground did and what they did about the cold. They must somehow live through the winter season without any ill effects because they were always around in the spring, summer and fall seasons. I just don't know what they do.

When I got to the barnyard and went through it over to the little house, there was Grandpa fixing our supper. I got undressed from the winter clothes and got ready to eat. Grandpa wanted to know where I had been. I told him where I had gone and what I had seen while there. He said that there were quite a few deer around in the immediate area. He saw them frequently and he wondered also if my little deer was among them. I said that the little deer would be fairly large by now. After all she was almost a year old and living quite well off the land, or she'd be back for bottle-feeding. He pretty much agreed with me but said that he hoped that I would get to see the little deer before the weekend and the end of the year.

Soon Christmas vacation was over and I had to go back home in town. I didn't like that very much but I made up my mind to make the best of it. Make the best of it I did, going to school every day and trying to enjoy the time with the other kids. It worked out that way, as long as I didn't let myself get too far away and thinking about the deer all the time. All of the kids wanted to know about the little deer. I told them that everything in the world has to grow some every year and that I had let it go hoping that it would come back to me some day. All of the kids were pretty sad about the little deer just as I was.

This routine went on until Easter time when we had another vacation scheduled, but because of the church schedule, I didn't get to go out to the farm. We were all in need of a good vacation by then so the Easter holiday was very welcome indeed. After the holiday we were all back in school, enjoying it as much as we could. The kids kept asking about the little deer and I told them that I didn't know any more than I did at Christmas time. They were disappointed with my answers but what could I say? I merely said that she would be back on her own some day when I least expected her to show up. That seemed to satisfy most of them but some of the others went on asking about the little deer every day. It got so that I wouldn't even answer them any more because it made me so sad just thinking about it. I just turned away and talked to some one else, it was a little rude of me but what else was I to do? I think that some of them are still mad at me today as I write this.

When summer came we were all ready for it with both arms pumping! Especially for me because summer meant that I could go to the farm again and really look around for the little deer. When the day came that school was let out for the last time that year we all shouted for joy, even the teachers who had patiently put up with our mischievous ways all year. We were all happy as could be, and we shouted it out to the world to hear. I for one let out a yell as loud as any one else and ran most of the way home. When I came into the apartment my Mother said, "What's the matter with you?" I said, "Not a thing. Not a thing."

The first full day of summer was still to be on Monday and I couldn't argue with that. The very next day Grandpa came to town as usual on his weekly trip to the barbershop and I got to ride along with him just like I used to in old the days. Boy was that ever nice. Wow! But I was alone, without Ronnie or any one else to spin me around in the barber chair. I said that little thing didn't matter too much, and went along anyhow. When Grandpa was done with his haircut he said for me to get in the chair and get mine cut, too. Up in the chair I got and the barber asked me, "What kind of a cut would you like?" I said, "Can you give me a crew cut, please." He started in to give me a crew cut and in a minute or so he said, "I can't give a crew cut, so I guess a butch cut will have to do you." I said, "OK with me I guess.

But you'll have to explain to my mother about the cut." He said, "OK he'd do it and to have my mother call him and he would explain it to her." When the barber was done with the cutting Grandpa said, "Andiamo," which meant 'Lets Go'.

We got into the Chevy coupe after Grandpa had paid the barber. Off we went down Railroad Street and then down 5th Avenue toward the Brooklyn Road. When we got to the Brooklyn Road we turned left and headed down the hill toward Brooklyn. We were on or way to get to Gambuci's Hardware Store. When we got there out of the coupe we jumped and went into the store. Inside we went around to the shelves and looked at the goods on display. Then Grandpa said, "Oh I need some gas too." Old Frank Gambuci went out to give us some gas and when he was through he came back inside. Young Frank Gambuci had died a few years later. Grandpa paid him and asked, "Has the package had come yet?" Frank Gambuci said, "I really didn't expect it to come for at least another month or so." Grandpa said, "They had better hurry and ship it because winter as only about four or maybe five months away."

We got back in the coupe, went around the block to get headed for Hibbing and we were on our way at last. While driving through Brooklyn I saw several kids from school and they all wanted to know how the little deer was. I shouted to them that I didn't know anything new yet and that I would tell them when something new came up. When we got to the store Grandma said that there had been two very big guys asking about us but she didn't know who they were. Grandpa said that they probably were two of the guys that had helped us lower the new house onto its foundation and not to worry about them.

With that he made his tour of the basement to check on the furnace, then up to the first floor to see that everything up there was ok. Then he went on up stairs, to get undressed, and to take his bath. It never ceased to amaze me how he managed to time it so well; to be at the bathtub, have it full of hot water just when he was ready to take his underwear off. After about an hour, soaking in the hot water, he would call me to go get some Fells Naptha soap for him to wash with. I always had a new bar ready for him by that time, and then I would proudly open the door and toss it in to him.

When his bath was done he would dry himself off and proceed to get dressed in his town clothes. With that accomplished, he would announce to everyone within shouting distance that he was off for places and things unknown, he would get down to the Chevy Coupe, and with or without permission, he would be on his route checking in on the Italian population of the community. If I were standing close by the door to the car, I would generally be invited along on the sojourn.

These trips into the community were of a fatherly, helpful nature and would entail giving advice on various topics, the most important of which was the winemaking preparations this time of year. The barrels had to be cleaned and thoroughly rinsed out with hot water, filled with the hot water right up to the top and left to sit for at least two weeks. That would ensure that there were no leaks whatsoever. A leak in a barrel would mean that that barrel was not good enough to be used for storage of the wine and had to be withdrawn from the whole process of wine making, and replaced with a beverage-tight barrel.

Grandpa would go from house to house in the Italian community, have a cup of coffee at the old timer's places, give his advice, give condolences where necessary, and then be off to the next household. Often there would be children, about my age to play with me. That was the lucky times that I enjoyed so very much and looked forward to every time that Grandpa said, "Andiamo!" Those were the times when the kids and I would get to play with one another to the fullest extent of the law.

A good example of that was Jimmy who was always home for us when we came. He and I would always run down to the frog pond near his house. Also close by was the popshop and Erickson's Lumber

Yard. Jimmy could talk for about three hours on any subject that you picked out. He was a surprising kid to say the least. Another exceptional example was the Heinig boys who were living just up the street about a block from Jimmie's house. They were always home and always wanted to play; they were so nice all the time. Grandpa used to like to go there too.

I especially enjoyed the visits that Grandpa would make to the older Italian men along his route, because it gave me an opportunity to watch Grandpa in action. It was always nice to know that Grandpa knew as much as he did about the winemaking process. He gave advice on every aspect of the trade from barrels to buying the right kind of grapes. This he did unreservedly at every opportunity, for Grandpa was not all bashful when it came to making wine. For instance, when we would go to the Sabini household he would always have to instruct the boys how to get the barrels ready for the wine making process. This was because the older Mr. Sabini was in a nursing home and the boys never learned the trade from their father. I guess that was because they lived in America now, and didn't have to know wine making. But they were always very loyal to their father and tried very hard to learn the trade. Grandpa could see this and made an extra effort for them every time. It made me very proud of My Grandpa too. After visiting the Sabini home, I always said, "That was very nice, Grandpa." and he would say, "You've always got to be good to other people, because you just never know what this life will bring the next time around." You know, he was right, and I've practiced that bit of advice religiously, generously, and unscrupulously.

When we were finished with his rounds of instruction we'd always head home by way of Garfield Street and would stop off at the County Court House to see the jailors and find out if there was anything that we could do for them. Since the occurrence with Mrs. Amis they had become fast friends with Grandpa, and always had a big 'Hello' for him.

Then we'd motor on up 2nd Avenue to Lincoln Street and turn west to get to the store. All I can say is that my Grandpa really knew a lot of people and they all came to know a little bit more about wine making.

The store was always a nice place to end our day, mostly because that's where our families lived and it was always nice to be with family. When we got to the store I raced upstairs to see my mom. She asked, "Are you going to the farm with Grandpa in the morning?" I said, "Sure, if is alright with you." Anything to get me out of her hair! I said, "I need some clean clothes." She replied, "I will have them ready for you in the morning." "May I go play with my friends?" I asked. She gave me her permission and I went outside to find them.

I soon found some of them over in the vacant lot beside Toivola's house. We got started on a football game and played most of the rest of the day. They all wanted to know about my little deer and what she was doing right then. I was honest about my friend, and I told them that I didn't know where she was and I didn't know if she would ever be back. That was quite a surprise to them. They all said that I should know where my two friends were all the time. I told them that I left the gate to the cage open for them all the time so that they could come and go as they pleased. I couldn't be keeping an eye on them all the time. The farm was different than the town and besides, I didn't want to be ever watchful.

Sunday, after church, my Mother wanted to know what I wanted to do. I said, "I want to go to the farm for the rest of the day." She said, "Don't you think you spend enough time at the farm? Your Dad and I hardly ever see you." "Oh," I said, "come out to the farm and you can see me any time." She let it drop. When Grandpa came by that afternoon I just got in the car and said, "Let's go." Off we went.

As excited as I was about getting to the farm it was really not quite as exciting as I had thought that it would be. Mostly because my two friends weren't at the farm any more and Spike the dog had told me that they were gone for sure. Anyway, I was just as excited as ever to be there at the farm and when we stopped the car I got out and ran up to the cage to see for sure that my two little pets were gone. What do you know! There they were alive and well. They seemed to be as excited to see me as I was to see them and came right over to me. I said, "Do you want a drink of milk? If you do follow me down to the little house and I'll get you some." Down the hill we all went and when Grandpa saw us together he smiled and smiled. He was almost as happy about the two of them being there as I was. Over at the little house we went into the basement to get the milk. After I finally got the two bottles filled and put the nipples on them I went upstairs to heat the milk and the two of them followed me. I was heating the milk and Grandpa was getting them a shovel full of bran. Talk about the servants getting served by the masters, well I declare! They deserved it all and much, much more!

When the milk was finally ready, I gave the first bottle to the deer. While doing this the rabbit came over to me and seemed to say, "I'd like mine, too, you old scoundrel." I gave the bottle to her and there I was feeding the two of them at the same time. It was quite a thrill for me, as it must have been for Grandpa too. When they had finished their milk they immediately went over to eat the bran that Grandpa had brought for them. While eating the bran they kept looking around as if they were expecting someone else to come in. But no one came in. They just went on eating till the bran was all gone. Then they stood in their places and waited as if some one else was coming to see them. We all, Grandpa included, stood there and soon, into the yard comes a car. Right behind that car was my Dad's car with both my Mom and Dad. In the first car were the three big guys who had helped to lower the new house down the foundation walls. It was like old home week with everyone talking at once and shaking hands all around not once but two or three times. Gee, but it was good to see them all again, even my Mom and Dad who I had just seen this morning.

The discussion grew lively and loud. I could see that this frightened my two friends. I knelt down between them and stroked each of them and talked gently to both of them. They were scared but they stayed by me. Then my Mom came over to see us. Then she said, "I can see why you always want to go to the farm now. Who are your little friends? Please introduce me to them." I said to my two friends, "This is my Mother you guys." The two of them seemed to understand me. The deer turned to her and the rabbit turned to her and I said, "You can pet them very gently, Mom." She did. The deer as well as the rabbit just stood there as though it was an everyday thing and let her touch them and be petted. I was so proud that I could have popped all the buttons off my shirt if I had had a button up shirt on.

The three big guys were just standing there watching all this quietly because Grandpa had told them no loud talking at all. Soon one of them asked if he could come over to see the deer up close so I said, "OK if you come slowly and don't make any noise." Which he did and the other two guys did too. Pretty soon, they were all crouched down and petting the two of them. I don't think that I have ever seen such smiles of happiness on anybody's faces as I saw on the three of them. It gave me such an amount of pleasure. In about fifteen minutes the deer started to pull away from them and I said, "It's OK, Just go if you want to," and the deer and the rabbit just went quite calmly like they were just out for a stroll in the moonlight. I was so proud of them! You could have hit me over the head with a big stick and I wouldn't have noticed it at all.

My New Friend Peaceful

The three big guys wanted know if we got the house down and cemented onto its foundation. Grandpa said for them to sit down and went down to the basement to get a little more vino to drink. They were all sitting down and drinking except my Mother. She was outside watching the deer and the rabbit eating more grass in the yard. I came outside too and stood by her. She Said, "Would you like to have a dog at home?" I said, "No, because then you would have to take care of it all the time, and what good would that be to me?" "I agree with you on that point for sure" she said. Besides I had a new baby brother just to keep her going all day and most of the night. His name was Tommy.

When it came time to go, all the men came out of the house into the yard. The three big guys wanted to know how I got the deer and the rabbit to come to me and to no one else. I replied that it was because I had fed them when they were very young and they remembered being treated with kindness and not shouting at all at them. They could do the same thing with a deer and a rabbit of the same age. All they had to do was to find the animals out in the cold when they were young enough to not care too much who picked them up or who fed them. Kind of a tough proposition, but that's what they had to do. "Oh" the three guys said, "you are entirely right when you say that it is kind of a tough proposition because it's so tough that we would never could make the grade. It is a good thing that there is a younger generation coming up to show us old duffers how it is done." With that they got into their car and started for home.

Meanwhile Mom and Dad were still there and were talking between themselves. They came over to where I was sitting and said, "Are you sure you wouldn't want a dog to live with at home?" Again I said, "Yes I'm sure. Because Mom would have to take care of it all the time I would be in school, and that wouldn't be fair to either Mom or the dog." They looked at one another and said, "I guess we'll just have to take the dog back then." With that decided, they said their good-byes, got into their car and started for home. The little deer came over to me and got under my hand so that my hand was resting on her back. I got the hint and started to pet her as I had before in the house. She was very appreciative of this and turned her head toward me, stretched out her head a little bit and gave my face a licking like it had never been licked before or since. Was I ever proud of that licking! I just quivered from my head down to my little toes.

I spent the rest of the day just petting my two friends and enjoying their company. Late that afternoon I fixed them another bottle and fed the two of them until the bottles were dry. Then I said to them that it was time to go to bed. With my having said that they turned round and started up the hill toward the cage. Darned if they didn't understand everything I said just as if they spoke and understood the English language. I was just amazed at the two of them. I couldn't help but mention it to Grandpa and he said that I had better go check on them to be sure that was where they did go. I couldn't understand why, but I went up the hill toward the cage and when I could see into the cage I saw the two of them standing inside the gate just looking around. I guess that answers the question from Grandpa about the animals understanding the language as I spoke it.

The rest of the month went by quickly with me at the farm and all. The month of August wasn't just another month. It was county fair month, and that took a lot of preparations. Among the chores that needed to be done were to go to the Italian booth at the fairgrounds, clean it up and paint it. There were a hundred and one things that were always in need of being done. It was with much anticipation that the work was done and the few of us boys that could understand the Italian language found ourselves working. Mrs. Farrucci was the queen of the restorers and what a queen she was. Always pushing the boys to do more work, even though they had already become terribly tired from doing their previous work chores.

Finally, the day of the fairs opening arrived and we got to go home and put on clean clothes after we had taken a bath, of course. When it came time for the beer truck to make a trip to the Fair Grounds I got to ride in the truck. What an honor that was! To ride in the beer truck and to deliver beer and pop to all the stands that needed beer and pop, was indeed a great thing. Surpassed only by the Man On the Flying Trapeze, to say the very least. We kids spent every hour of every day at the fair. Mrs. Farrucci saw to it that we were given spaghetti lunches and plenty of it too along with all the milk we needed to quench our thirst. Never let it be said that we were loafers when it came to eating either, because we would eat every piece if spaghetti that Mrs. Farrucci gave us, and the bread and milk too.

With the County Fair behind us we had to return to the farm and our two little friends. This we did with gusto, not unlike the cry of the booth barkers at the fair. Getting back to the farm, when we did at last arrive at the farm, it was much the same as when we left it. The little house was still there as was the barn, the new house, the wind charger for the batteries, and all the animals. We had lucked out again and nothing was missing. I wondered about my two little friends. Were they still here also or did they take off again for parts unknown? It could be either way. When I got up to the cage, they were no place to be seen at all. The cage was empty of their two bodies as it was empty of the fancy birds that resided there before them. I called Spike again to come and look around for me. Spike went through his, by now old, routine and wound up on the top of the grain shed hill looking off into the sunset.

I was deeply disappointed to say the least. I wondered where could they be. All kind of visions went through my head. I envisioned them on the trail together trying to get over a big log and trying to get across the creek somewhere. I just had an unending series of mental pictures of the two of them stuck somewhere out in the woods trying to get back. I went to bed and lay down but I didn't sleep for quite a while. When I finally did go to sleep it was with their pictures in my head and I dreamed of them all night. The next day was a Sunday and I had to go to church so Grandpa gave me a ride into town where I got a bath and clean clothes. Then my Mom and Dad said that it was time to go to church so I jumped in the car ahead of them and was already to go to church. After church my Mom said, "Would you like to go out to eat?" I said, "Sure I would." So off we went to South Hibbing, as Alice was called now, to a new place on Howard Street called the Howard Lounge. When we got there the owner, a Mr. Fotopopulous took us to a booth and asked if it was all right. My Dad said that it was fine, and Mr. Fotopopulous said, "Have the beer truck stop by in the morning." My Dad said, "I'd be happy to do that, Tom" and we went on to eat our meal. After we were done we got in the car and began driving home.

On the way we stopped at a very nice house and started to go in. My Dad went first and then my Mom and I came last. When my Dad opened the gate I heard a group of dogs barking and I ran ahead of my Mom to see the dogs. They were beautiful, all nicely grown up and smooth coated. One in particular came to me and wanted to be petted. I broke down and petted her a little. She liked that part a lot. I petted her from then on while we were there. Gee, she was a good dog and she liked me it seemed for sure. Then I started to run around and the dog came after me running when I ran and stopping when I stopped. Gee was she every bit of the dog that I wanted but she was a town dog, not a farm dog and wouldn't fit into the farm life for sure. My Mom said, "Do you like the dog? Would you like to have her home with you?" I said, "No, and you know why I don't." "Oh," she said, "if that is the only reason, you can forget it, because it would be all right with me if we had her home."

That little episode sort of stunned me completely and I didn't know what to say. I said, "OK. If you want the dog get her then," and let it go at that. My Dad said that they would come back that afternoon to see about the dog. Then the owner came out of the house and said Hi to my Dad, and Dad said that he would be back after lunch to pick up the dog. That pretty much ended all the negotiations between them and we got into the car. We drove right back home then and waited for Grandpa to come and pick me up to go to the farm. We didn't have to wait very long, only about an hour or so and there he was. I ran down the stairs and out to the car to meet him. He said to get in the coupe and sit down, which I did until he got in and got ready to go. Right then I jumped up on the seat and stood up on the seat so I could look out and be seen by one and all along our route. It was off to the farm we went just putting along our route to South Hibbing, and the Dupont Road.

We started off down the Dupont Road going along quite nicely when all of a sudden a man got out in front of us and waved us down. We stopped the car and he came over to Grandpa's window and said that we are to turn around and go back to the store. He didn't know why, just that we were to go back to the store right away. We turned around and headed back to the store, and when we got to Howard Street in South Hibbing we drove along to 3rd Avenue and turned right to get back up to town. When we got back to the store my Dad said, "Wait a minute for the dog" and went into the store. He came back with the dog that was so nice this morning that I had petted so much. I was a little bit surprised, but my Dad said, "You'll have to take her to the farm because we don't have room for her here." Grandpa said, "Put her in the rumble seat and tie her down good." My Dad did as he was requested and tied the dog down.

That was the beginning of a great friendship that lasted for many years. It was something I approved of whole-heartedly. I was concerned though that my Mother would have to take care the dog in the fall when I came back to town to go to school and said so to my Dad.

He said not to worry my little head one little bit about it because we would be moving to the upstairs of the popshop by then and my Mom would have plenty of room to take care of her. That sounded all right to me so I said OK. Then we were off to the farm again but this time Grandpa took the Brooklyn Road and turned left on to the highway when we got to the Kittsville turn off. He turned to go through Kittsville and out the other side of the location and continued going on the Kitsville Road.

He crossed the highway and went down the Kittsville Road toward Wilpen. We continued on our way and the dog seemed to be awfully curious about our surroundings. She was looking all around us. She was just curious is all you could say about her, just curious. Next came Wilpen and the bridge over the railroad tracks. The dog was most curious about the train going by on the tracks. Then came the ride over the trace where the new house was towed. This part of the ride was the most interesting to the dog. She tried her best to get untied and up off the seat in the rumble seat in an effort to look around at the sights. She kind of whined when she couldn't get off the seat but she kept looking at all the surrounding landscape anyhow.

We soon came to the farm and the gate in the fence. I got out of the car to open the gate for the car and to close it after the car had gone through. From here on it was easy going on the gravel that Grandpa had laid down for the new house to be towed over to the foundation where it now rested. The dog was most curious about everything on the farm. When the car came to a stop, she was even more curious about her surroundings. I got out, and I got up by the rumble seat to get the end of her rope that was tied to the seat and said come on to the dog. She was more than just willing to come. She was over anxious to come and bounded out of the seat and onto the ground. Then she heard Spike bark his greeting to one and all. Her ears perked up to hear better. She stopped with one paw raised and looked around. By that time Spike had come around the corner from his doghouse and the two of them saw each other at the same instant.

Spike looked at the dog, the dog looked a Spike, and the two of them didn't bark or whine or anything. I just stood there next to the dog, Grandpa got out of his door of the car and just stood where he was. He was waiting for Spike to get angry because we had another dog with us, but that didn't happen the way we thought it would. Spike just walked over to where the dog was standing, came up to her nose to nose. The dog was just sitting down quietly watching Spike's every move. Finally the two of them seemed to have signed a peace treaty and soon were busy going through the welcoming committee of smelling each other and checking each other out. That took care of the arrival of the dog on the farm. However, tomorrow would be another day and we could only wait and see.

By this time Grandpa had his afternoon chores to do so he got busy doing them. I had the dog stay with me for the remainder of the afternoon in the little house so that she could get used to it and it wouldn't be so strange to her. She seemed to like that part enough and stayed by me willingly for the rest of the day. I couldn't help but wonder what she would think of the popshop when we moved in there. I had all kinds of visions of what the dog would do from barking because she liked it to her running away. But I said, why borrow trouble ahead of time, wait and see what takes place. Grandpa came in after his chores were done to begin getting supper ready. I was wondering what I could feed the dog and came to the conclusion the table scraps would probably be enough, but tomorrow I'd have to figure something out for sure. Grandpa and I ate our supper with dog looking on very disappointedly. When we were finished eating I started to clean up the dishes and saved all the scraps for dog. When I was done washing I took the saved scraps and put them into a tin plate type of dish, then put it down on the floor. Only then did the dog come over and eat. It was obvious that she was well trained.

Then I sat down to read the paper that grandpa had brought, but it wasn't much fun just pretending I could read. Maybe by the end of next school year I'd be able to read some at least. I went outside and up to the cage for another look just in case they had returned. My friends hadn't come back yet so I just walked around a little and took the dog for a little walk around the barnyard. She stayed right at my heel and just walked along at my speed. I could tell that we were going to be good friends and I was happy about that too. By that time it was beginning to get dark so I started back for the little house and looked forward to a good night's rest. When I got back to the little house I went right in and the dog followed me in. Then I got ready for bed and she stayed right with me until I got in the little bed of mine. She stood and watched the whole time and when I got under the covers she came over to me and whimpered a little like she wanted to get in with me. I took one of the blankets off my bed place and laid it on the floor for her. She came over to it, sniffed it a little bit and must have approved of the smell, I guess, because she lay down on it. As far as I know she went right to sleep, as did I, quite soon after I lay flat.

Fight!

It seems like it wasn't but a couple of days and it was school again. The dog and I had fun for the last few days of summer vacation. We became inseparable playmates and were together every minute of the day. So good was our friendship that she slept with me each night. She was there early in the morning helping me with the breakfast dishes and tagged along with me when I went up to the cage to check on the missing two friends from out in the wild woods, so to speak. The deer and the rabbit were still gone but the dog smelled their presence and let me know it the minute it came to her. She went all around in the cage with her good old nose doing the sniffing and checking out every sliver of grass in the corner that we had placed for the deer.

The dog would spend a few minutes running from point to point with her nose going a hundred miles an hour, and then she would stop the moving about and look up at me as if to say, "Where did you put them?" I said that they were gone and I didn't know if they would ever be back. The dog seemed to understand every word that I said and she looked so sad to me. I didn't know if I should smile or cry. I just stood there and said they're gone and I don't know where they are, but if they were to come back I would welcome them with open arms and full milk bottles.

Soon enough the summer months and final days were over and gone, and I had to move back into town as did the dog. We had become fast friends and were almost inseparable. Where ever I went the dog was sure to go too. But I was a little troubled, what name should I call the dog? I just couldn't keep calling her "the dog" could I? I had a contest with myself to see who could come up with a better name. The first one to come up with a name would get the next Saturday off from school and would have the whole weekend free as a prize. That sounded pretty good to me, so I began immediately to try to think of a name. Of all the names in the world, I couldn't think of one that was acceptable. I couldn't think of a name that was good enough. She was Rust colored with white shoes or stockings, as you will, about her feet. She was quite a different dog in many respects from the ordinary run-of-the-mill dog. The more I thought about it, the harder the problem became. I kept coming back to the word, "Different."

The more I thought about it the more the word seemed to fit her. "Different," I said to myself over and over again. I started calling her Different and soon she started to respond to the name even more than I could hope for. I'd say "Here Different" and she'd come trotting over from where ever she was at the time, and always looking for a handout. She always expected me to have a goodie or two stuffed away in one of my pockets. When she wouldn't find a goodie she would mope around like the last days of summer for sure. She always let me know about it too. She would bark at me with no restraint whatsoever until I could get her calmed down again.

After school started, I was walking to the old McGoleric School up on Rail Road Street, which was quite a ways across town. I said that we'd better move into the popshop pretty soon or there would be one little boy that refused to go to school any more. In a week or so my Mom said that on Saturday the men would be here to help us move. Hooray, Hooray! On Saturday I was up earlier than normal, about 6:00 o'clock, and looking outside for the men. My Mom was a little unhappy about the time but she didn't say too much to me about it.

As it turned out, we needed the time just to get things ready for the men to come and move us. First thing I know there was Brooklyn

Joe, one of the guys that was going to help move us. Pretty soon Roy showed up with another guy and we got started with the move. We had so much stuff to move that we were still moving it in about 1:00 o'clock. I think it took us two loads and we were all moved from Lincoln Street down to the popshop at the end of Fifth Avenue and McKinley Street. I said Hooray again because now I was closer to school by at least a couple of blocks and could walk almost all the way up there using the path in the "cow pasture" as we called it. From Washington Street it was only another four blocks to the school. Joey and I would be able to walk it from Washington Street together as we agreed to do.

On Monday I was already to go right after breakfast. I started out about 7:00 AM and got to Joey's house long before 8:00 AM. He was all ready to go and he came right out and we started right away. We got up on the hill on Sellers Street and we met up with Pat also on his way to school. Turned out to be old home week, and we hadn't even gotten to school yet. We got there soon enough as it was, and Different was happy to see all the kids in the schoolyard. When we all went into the school, Different figured that she should come in to. I had a heck of a time getting her to stay outside. She just didn't want to. I guess she was so attached to me that she just figured that she had to be inside. At noontime there she was still waiting for me by the door. When I came out she jumped up on me and knocked me down. All the kids thought that was pretty cool.

When I got home for lunch I tied her up with the chain that I had just for that purpose. I told my Mom not let her off the chain until after school was out at 3:30 and I told her why. She said OK, but I could tell from the way she said it that she had every intention of letting the dog off the chain as soon as I was gone. I left to go back to school as soon as I had eaten my lunch. I kept worrying all afternoon about the dog and kept wondering if she was loose or not. When 3:30 o'clock, came I was ready for the bell and started for the door when a little boy ahead of me let out a shout of alarm. I couldn't imagine why he was shouting that way before he got out of the building. When I got up by the boy I could see why. He was dressed the same as I was with the same shirt and color of pants, and there was Different standing over him wondering just what the heck she had done. What she had done was to knock down the wrong kid is all that she had done. That was the stick that broke my back. That's for sure.

I took the dog by the collar and wouldn't let go of her until I got all the way home. She knew that she had done something wrong and kept trying to get away from me on the whole ten blocks getting home. I didn't let her get away from me again. I just kept a close hold on her collar until we got home and then I put the chain on her again so she would have to stay home. Then I went up stairs to my Mom and asked her when she had let the dog loose. She said that it was a darn shame to keep a fine dog such as this one on the chain for the whole afternoon. She had gone down and turned it loose about 2:00 o'clock and the dog just took off in the direction of the school. I said that I would take care of it soon as supper was done with. In the mean time my Dad came home and saw the dog chained up to the building and wanted to know why. I told him the whole story about the poor kid laying on the ground with the dog standing on top of him smelling him like there was no tomorrow.

I told my Dad that I would go down, give the dog a good lecturing, and then I would set her free to go wherever she wanted to go. First, we had supper and after that my Mom did up the dishes, fixed up my baby brother, and took him out for a ride with my Dad. I went downstairs and started to talk to the dog. You could tell that she felt pretty bad about this afternoon just by looking at her. She was sitting on her rump with her front legs stiff out in front of her and her head was way down by her front paws. She was a pretty sad looking dog at that and even I felt sorry for her. Just because I felt sorry for her, I knew that I couldn't let her get away with it. I started talking to her quietly telling her that she did a bad, bad thing today and she would have to be chained up every day if she did it again. In the mean time I would consent to her being off the leash if she would be good and behave herself. She looked at me with those great big beautiful eyes and I just melted away to nothingness. There was nothing I could do. I was deactivated for sure. I left her on the leash for about an hour and then I came back and took off the chain. She was real happy about that move and licked my face and stayed right by my side.

The very next morning about 9:00 o'clock, Jimmy and some of the other guys showed up needing another player for their ballgame and asked me to come and play with them, so I said sure. We went to the ballpark across Brooklyn road and up on the top of the leveled out ground that the city had made for a ballpark. It was just that, a flattened out area with crab grass growing in clumps all over it. But it was a ballpark of sorts, and we'd always use it as such. We had bases that we had made ourselves and two dugouts that the city had put in for the teams. We didn't have any organized groups of ball players; just scrub teams that the gangs would make up each time. Today it was the Lincoln Street bunch and the McKinley Street bunch that were getting together for about the first time in their existence. It had the promise of a fight for sure by the time we had nine innings in.

My dog was along and followed me everywhere I went, even out on the field. She lay down and watched the whole group of us guys playing ball. When a ball was hit and came her way she immediately ran after it. I took her by the collar and said, "You've got to behave and that's all there is to it!" Then I took her over to the dugout and made her sit down while I went back out to the game and started to play again. The rest of the boys were all giving me the razz about the dog but it didn't bother me a bit. I just went on playing ball. Every once in a while I would look over at the dugout and would see my dog just standing on her hind feet with her front paws on the edge of the dug out.

When the game got to about the sixth inning the boys were talking pretty loudly between themselves and pretty soon it came to fighting between them. My dog came out of the dugout and raced over to the two boys that were fighting and jumped right into the middle of the fight. She grabbed one arm in her teeth and knocked the boy down. Then she got up and grabbed the other boy by the arm in her teeth and knocked him down. All this she did in the twinkling of an eye before anybody could interfere. She just stood looking down at the two boys, standing at attention after she had them both down on the ground. She was just ready to get the first of them that moved a muscle. I came right over to the place where the fight had been and looked to see who was on the ground. It turned out be two of the boys who I thought had always gotten along with one another quite well. I said to the dog, "Stay", and to the two boys I said, "You can get up now, but please shake hands and show the dog that you are all right. the two boys did all of that and said that they were sorry to each other and to the rest of us for fighting and the two of them came over to my dog and petted her and said that they were sorry.

Someone said that he was hungry and it must be close to noon. We pretty much agreed to get together again that afternoon so we could to finish the game. I thought that we had already finished the game, after all we had played for about twelve innings and the score wasn't tied up. But anyway, we all agreed to come right back after lunch to continue the game. We all broke up and went on our respective journeys home.

I kept thinking all the way home that I needed a new name for the dog, but I just couldn't think of one. All during lunchtime I thought and thought, but I just couldn't seem to think of an appropriate name for the dog. I asked my Mom what should I name her. She thought the name I had used on her was good enough and wasn't too much help at all. Then all of a sudden the name came to me. It had its foundation in what the dog had done that morning during the fight between the two boys. "Peaceful," was the right name for her. I said it over and over to myself, just to memorize it so that I wouldn't get it wrong at the wrong time. After lunchtime I started in calling her

Peaceful and she didn't mind the name change at all, she didn't come when I first used the new name but she'd get used to it soon enough.

Around 2:00 o'clock the boys all showed up to continue on with the game that we had started this morning. The first thing the Lincoln Street bunch wanted was, they wanted to pick sides. We all sat down at one of the dugout benches and we let two guys, one from each gang, pick their teams. We were all sitting around and we got pretty chummy by the time the teams were picked. This was one of the things that the city thought should happen at the ballpark. It worked out well just the way it was supposed to. Then we started the game all over again, with the two new sides, and even liked the arrangements. I wound up on the McKinley Street team because I was a little guy and couldn't hit my own hat floating in a barrel with a broom. I'd show them. Just who did they think they all were anyhow?

When my turn came up for batting I hit the first pitch real hard. The ball sailed over all the heads out in the field and went out beyond the playing field into the grassy area behind center field for a home run. "Little Guy" who "just couldn't hit his hat floating in a barrel" had showed them a thing or two, I thought to myself as I rounded third base headed for home. Everybody from both teams had to go out and look for the darned ball. After about an hour of hard looking I was the lucky guy to find the ball and it had traveled about 800 or 1000 feet after it got rolling down the hill. After that I was a pretty popular guy with everyone asking just how I got a hit on that ball anyhow.

So went the fall days, and school days too for that matter. Even my dog "Peaceful" was peaceful too. Then I learned that Ronnie wasn't coming home as I had figured and that threw a monkey wrench into all my plans for the winter months. I kept on going out to the farm every chance I got but never did see my little deer or rabbit again. That part saddened me too, more than even I liked to admit. The days kept on sliding by and pretty soon it was Easter Sunday and we all went to church. It wouldn't be but a couple of months more. Summer would be on our doorstep pretty soon. Sure enough even Peaceful could tell the time of year because she started to get friskier than ever. Then one day all the snow and ice were gone for sure, and spring had sprung. There wasn't anything more to do but bide our time and drum our fingers until they almost fell off.

Soon, school was over and we could "summer it up" all we wanted too. Most of us wanted to do just that. I for one couldn't wait to get out to the farm to get involved again in the chores around the place. To see the chickens in their coop and to see how they were getting along since we covered up the holes in the walls. That day came on a Saturday and my Grandpa picked me up to go for a shave and a haircut. Up the street to Roseskes shop we went and I jumped out of the car when we were parked at the curb in front of the barbershop. Grandpa came around the front of the car and we went into the shop. When we got inside Mr. Roseske said that I had grown a bit since he saw me last. I knew that he was just passing the time of day because I had been in to get a cut last week. This is the kind of thing that really got to me. Always there was good deal of small talk that didn't mean a thing to anyone. Seemed like a true waste of time to me. Anyway, Grandpa got his weekly shave and monthly haircut. The two of them, Grandpa and Mr. Roseske, talked all the time about business while I just sat in a waiting chair and did nothing but listen in. Soon it was time to go and grandpa paid the bill and we went out to the coupe to leave. Grandpa asked as we were getting into the car, "Where should we go today?" I said, "Any place is fine with me." Then he started the coupe and took off.

I just rode along for the ride, I guess, because I didn't know at all where we were headed. We went through South Hibbing as it was now called instead of "Alice", as it was named before. We went out on 1st Avenue to the south end of town and then down, across the highway to the extended part of 1st Avenue and on to the south for quite a distance. All of a sudden we came to a four way stop sign at the intersection of 1st avenue and county road B.

Across county road B sat Pauleys farm where all the chickens were grown. Grandpa crossed the county road and went into the farm. He said. "You wait here." and got out of the car to talk to a man that I assumed was Mr. Pauley. They spent quite some time talking and finally the man turned toward one of the buildings and went inside. Grandpa followed along behind him. They were gone for quite a while and when they came back they each had a case about four feet long, about three feet across and about one foot deep. They put them in the rumble seat and tied them in. Grandpa could see that I was just boiling over with a million and one questions. He said that it was a new bunch of chickens for the farm. What did he need a new bunch of chickens for I asked myself.

I figured that some of the hens were not the best egg producers and he was replacing them with the new stock. But I'd have to wait until we got to the farm to ask him. That day it seems that he was going right back to the farm with the chickens in the boxes in the rumble seat. when we got back to town we drove right on up First Avenue all the way up to North Hibbing, as it was now called, and stopped at the store. There we went in to say goodbye and give Grandpa a chance to change back into his farmer's garb. With this done, and the week's groceries loaded up in the car, we were ready to take off. We went down the street past the Lincoln school, down to McKinley Street and down the Brooklyn Road. Then off we went on the highway to the Rock Lawn Dairy road and down that road for seven miles to the cutoff Highway at Wilpen. We crossed the Highway and got onto the trace headed for the farm. We had gotten to the brink of the hill when Peaceful let out a bark. I couldn't understand why she would give just a single bark.

When I looked out of the side window I understood. There was a deer just off the road just standing there watching us with her head up and ears pointed toward us. I said to Grandpa, "Do you suppose that is my deer?" he said, "I don't know but why she would be standing there watching us if she wasn't?" Then I said, "Can I go see

Grandpa?" and he said, "Yes, of course." But what would I do with Peaceful? I didn't go to see. We just took off down the hill of the trace to the gate. I got out there and went over to open the gate, and it was then that I saw the deer running down the hill to us. Grandpa saw her too and said very quietly to remain stationary as I stood by the gate. I just stood there ever so quietly not making a sound or moving in any way. When the deer got to our immediate area she slowed down to a walk and came over to me. I was so excited that I didn't know what to do. I just stood there and looked at her. She kept coming over to me and reached up her neck and head so she could lick my face.

With that Grandpa started the car moving through the gate and Peaceful started barking. Even that didn't seem to scare the little deer, which incidentally was a little taller than I remembered her. I was just going over to close the gate when Peaceful set up a fuss to be let out of the car. I moved over to where the car was sitting and said, "Be quiet Peaceful and then I'll let you get out." She quieted right down. I said to the deer, "We have a new friend." and leaned over to open the car door. When Peaceful saw me open the door she came out slowly, carefully almost, with her eye on the deer and me. When she was on the ground she walked over to the deer and me. She put her face up to the deer's face and she licked it. The deer didn't know what to think. She didn't know if she should lick Peaceful back or what and she looked up at me. I said to go ahead and lick Peaceful back. Pretty quick she did just that and the dog didn't know whether she was afoot or horseback. When the deer stopped licking Peaceful, Peaceful stopped licking the deer. I said to Grandpa to go ahead and have a bottle ready in about ten minutes or so, and I would walk back. He took off right away and left me sitting with my two friends. That was all right because the two of them were really hitting it off in fine style. That didn't leave any thing for me to do except walk back to the farm.

Anyway, there I was with my two best friends, my dog, Peaceful, and the little deer. Together, the three of us walked back to the little house. It was only fitting that I go into the basement of the house and fix a bottle for the deer and take it upstairs to warm it up. Both Peaceful and the deer came along on both trips. When the milk was ready I began to feed the deer and Peaceful looked on with much curiosity, she just couldn't figure out what we were doing with this feeding business. When the bottle was empty I fed her the other bottle and Peaceful got really curious about that maneuver too. After the second bottle was done, I went out to get the bran for the deer and left the two of them together in the house alone. I don't know what I expected from either of them. It could have been any thing at all.

When I got back to the house, there they were both sitting down with their fore feet out straight down in front holding them up, nose to nose. I just wished that I had a camera to take a picture of the two of them. I put the little shovel of bran down on the floor and just stood and watched the two of them. The little deer went right to the bran while Peaceful just watched until the deer got over to the bran and started to eat. Then Peaceful went over there too and took a mouthful of the bran and tried to eat it to, but she started to choke up on it and tried to cough it out but she couldn't make it come out. She ran outside and down to the creek and stuck her nose in the water. I decided that she would be all right and stayed in the house with the little deer.

That had generally turned out fairly well except for Peaceful getting all choked up on the bran and drinking half the creek full of water to get it down, I was quite satisfied. It made my feelings about the whole situation seem totally insignificant when I saw what the little deer did next. She came over to Peaceful and licked her on the face. If I hadn't seen it happen right in front of me, I wouldn't have believed it in a thousand million years. Even then, I'd have to see it to believe it. Just about then, Grandpa came into the house and said that it was about time for supper and he started to search out things for the meal. I got up and set the table and my two friends just stayed where they were and watched me. When the meal was ready we both sat down to eat. My two friends stayed in the room watching both of us quite closely until we were done. Then when I got up they both came over to me and I petted both of them. It was time to clean up, so I went over to do the dishes and put them away. I remembered that I had not fed Peaceful so I got the food that was left and put it on a plate and I took it to her.

She ate like it was going out of style until she had her plate clean, when she looked up at me, as if to say, "You got any more, pardner?" I said, "I'm sorry but there ain't no more. You would eat us out of house and home if I gave you half a chance." With that I went outside, followed by my two friends. I said to the deer, "You can go up to the cage now if you like" and away she went on up the hill to her cage and Peaceful just sat and watched. This went on for about five minutes and then up the hill toward the cage goes Peaceful, and in about ten minutes down Peaceful came. I guess she was satisfied that the deer was all right for the night. That was good and all right with me too. I went into the little house and sat down. Peaceful went the other way over by Spike's doghouse. She stayed over there for about ten minutes and came back to the little house.

It was time for sleep and I got undressed and into my bed with Peaceful in beside me as well. But sleep didn't come too soon. I lay there awake for at least three hours thinking about the coming summer months. I just thought about all the time I'd have to roam around free and easy, to go wherever I pleased, whenever I pleased, to spend each day as it should be spent, being kind to all my friends and being nice to those people about me. Then splendid, comforting, helpful sleep came unassisted.

My New Friend, the Blue Jay

When I awoke in the morning it was barely light out and I couldn't sleep any more. Peaceful was still sleeping, so I let her be and crawled out of bed ever so gently so as not to awaken her, got dressed and went outside. There was Spike sleeping on the doorstep so I stepped over him quietly and got down off the porch of the little house and into the yard.

I snuck away without making a sound until I was up on top of the wind charger hill and then I could walk as I usually did. Away I went walking up the grain-shed hill and down the far side to the near side of the pasture fence. I climbed over the fence and went up to the woodchucks' dens next to the railroad fence. There was no activity here either, so I just looked around and started to go over to the potato hill by the back way. Then I spotted a beautiful blue jay bird flitting its way through the trees. I guess that it must have thought that I was a tree; because when I had my arm outstretched it flew right to it and landed on my forearm. I was so surprised that I couldn't move a muscle and just stood there and watched it sing its song. Pretty it was, too. I held my arm straight out from my shoulder and turned ever so slowly to my left to continue on my way. The Blue Jay set up an alarmed sort of vocal sound that I couldn't ignore so I stopped my turning around and just waited for the bird to begin singing again. In a couple of minutes it started in singing again. Was it ever beautiful!

I guess that the bird became one of my friends too and I loved it so. I began moving off to go to the potato patch hill the back way and the bird just came along with me, singing its song all the time as it flew along with me. I was so surprised that you could have knocked me over with a leaf. When I got to the potato patch here came Spike and Peaceful up the hill to meet me. Now how in the heck did they know where I was anyhow? I don't know if it was instinct or a bit of shrewd guessing on their part, but they found me for sure. It smelled pretty bad around the chuckholes from the dead chucks that we had left in their holes previously. There weren't any chucks around at all. Even the two dogs didn't want to stay around the place and ran down the hill to wait for the blue jay bird and me to come down.

Gosh! But this was just great, having so many good friends that I could count on all the time. There were the little deer, Spike, Peaceful, and "Bluie" for the blue jay, which were there just for the asking. I don't know of any other boy that had so many good friends even though I thought and thought about it. No, there just wasn't one. The two dogs were especially watchful when the little deer was around and they also came to know the Blue Jay bird quite well. They knew the bird well enough to tell the difference between the birds when they flew around the farm.

The rest of the summer went as well as could be expected, with the bird especially. Every morning when I'd come out of the little house it was there, singing away happily. The deer was growing by leaps and bounds, visible to one and all just for the looking. I began to have some mixed up feelings about the deer. I didn't know if keeping her here was such a good idea or not. I was beginning to have the pangs of separation anxiety just thinking about her growing up so fast. I kept looking for her to be gone for good one day down the line. I really expected it almost every day when I got up and was always so happy when I found her there again each day.

I felt the same about Bluie. It had been really amazing how the two dogs had accepted the bird and how Bluie had accepted them. I'll tell you that it was without a doubt the nicest arrangement that anybody could want for his or her animals. With the dogs looking out for the rest of the group, I couldn't ask for any thing more. Summer turned into fall and more school lay ahead. I had to leave my little menagerie and move into town not knowing if they would be there when I got back in the next summer or not. It was an awful teary some goodbye that I had to go through. I still would be able to come out to the farm on some weekends though. So all was not lost for sure.

Peaceful

Taking "Peaceful" with me was, of course, a foregone conclusion. She was happy about the move and the prospect of seeing so many of the kids that I played with everyday. Of course, they too were happy to see Peaceful and behaved around her because they knew about the fighting incident between the two boys. She was nosey as ever and wanted to be with me all the time. She went to school with me every-day and always wanted to come into the room. I had a heck of a time trying to keep her out of the classroom. I finally went up to the sister who was our teacher and asked her if she could come into the room. She said "Certainly not! This is a school not a pet shop!" I said "Then I can't come to school here either." With that I left the school and went outside to the playground. It took the nun a couple of minutes to catch her breath after that little exchange I guess.

Poor Sister Michael couldn't say a thing until I got out to the play-ground. Then she said, "Now you get back into school this minute or don't ever come back here again". Those were pretty strong words and even Peaceful seemed to know it because she was sitting with her head held way down between her front paws. I decided to go back in the school and went reluctantly. I got Peaceful to stay outside but it was much against her better judgment. It's a good thing that it was a Friday, because when I got out of school in the afternoon I immedi-ately ran home and asked my mother if could go to the farm with Grandpa tomorrow. She said it would be OK but right now I had to take a bath.

Into the bathroom I went, got undressed, and drew the bath water. I got into the tub and got all soaked up. I got the washcloth and bar of soap and scrubbed all over, and I mean I really scrubbed. When I was done I called my mom and told her so. She came in the bathroom and looked me over pretty good, pronounced me clean and began to dry me off. After she was done drying me I ran into the bedroom to get me some clean clothes. After I got dressed, down the stairs I went and outside.

Where was my dog? I called "Here Peaceful! Here Peaceful!" but she didn't come. I whistled and whistled for her and she still didn't come. I went around the building and didn't see her any place. I was at a loss looking for Peaceful, not finding her anywhere. Just then as I got out in front of the building again I saw a woman walking in from the Brooklyn Road carrying something in her arms.

At first I didn't think anything about it, just stopped to see what she was carrying. As she got closer I could see that she was carrying an animal of some kind. When she got close to me I could see that she was carrying a dog. The dog looked lifeless. The woman was saying over and over, "I'll never drive again. I'll never drive again!" It was my dog Peaceful that she was carrying. I ran over to her and said, "What happened?" She said, "The dog just ran in front of me and I couldn't stop the car." "Please," I said. "Just give her to me and I'll take her from here. She's my dog. I live right here." She handed me the dead Peaceful. I took her in my arms and stumbled a little because she was so heavy. I turned toward the popshop and started to walk. The tears were just streaming down my face. So much so that I couldn't see where I was going. The woman came over to me and said, "Are you going to the popshop building?" "Yes," I replied, and she guided me over to the front door. She opened the door and I went inside. I couldn't make it up the stairs and sat down on the bottom stair. The woman stayed with me and pretty soon my mom opened the stair top door.

My mom was curious and said, "What are you doing?" Then she saw the woman, and me crying away like there was no tomorrow. She came right down the stairs. Then she saw the reason that I was crying and why the woman was crying. She wanted to know what had happened. The woman said that she was driving on the Brooklyn Road and the dog ran right out in front of her car. She couldn't stop the car in time and hit the dog.

My mom said, "I hope you've got good insurance. That is a very expensive dog that you killed." The woman said, "I'll have my husband come over this evening and give you a check for the dog." With that my mom said for me to go upstairs and she invited the woman to also come up stairs for a cup of coffee. I just left the dog lie there and went on up stairs. The woman and my mom came up stairs too. They had a cup of coffee and talked an awful lot.

That was about it for my dog. She was dead and there wasn't anything I could do about it. She was gone forever and I would never be able to even pet her again. I just went to my room and cried my eyes out for hours. I was still there when my dad came in at suppertime and wanted to know about the dog. I told him as much as I knew about the situation and said that the woman had said that her husband would come over this evening to write a check for the dog.

"We've got to do something with the dog." My dad said, and I said, "Let's bury her out in front of the popshop in the little grass area that nobody uses at all". My Dad said, "That's a good idea, Joey. Let's go get the job done now". The two of us went down the stairs and I picked up Peaceful and carried her outside. My dad went into the garage area and got two shovels and came out to the grassy area. "Let's start in with the digging," my Dad said, and we started in digging a grave for Peaceful. I was never so lonely in all my life, but we got the hole dug in about an hour. Then it was time to set Peaceful in it. I picked up the dog and laid her in the hole, along with a whole torrent of tears. I then stood up and said the "Our Father" prayer. I don't know if I got all the words right or not, but at least I felt somewhat better about it all.

We had to shovel all the dirt back into the hole to cover up Peaceful and I said to my Dad, "Please let me do the covering up of Peaceful." Then he said, "All right, Joey. Go ahead and do the cover up job. I'll be right inside if you need me for anything at all." So I went ahead with the covering up job with some big tears in my eyes while I did the job. It took me about two hours to do the cover up job but I lasted that long and had a little mound of dirt on top of the grave. This I patted down nicely with the shovel and said another "Our Father" prayer over the grave. Then I went back up to the apartment and I went into my room to lie down.

Headstone

All I could think about was my dog Peaceful. Seems like every thought in my mind came up with Peaceful. I just lay in my room and looked at the ceiling for the whole night. I kept going over all the good times that we had had together. Seems like I couldn't even come up with one bad day ever. That made me so sad that I couldn't even find the right clothes to wear the next morning. My mother had to come in and help met to dress.

When I asked my mom where dad went she was very hesitant to say, just as if it were a big secret and I wasn't supposed to know. After breakfast, which I couldn't eat at all, my dad came in and said for me to get ready because we were going places. I couldn't really guess where he had in mind at all. I got up from the table and said that I was ready now. He asked my mom, "Ellen are you ready yet?" She said, "Wait a minute and I will be." She was getting my baby brother Tommy ready to go to. I figured this must be a big deal if mom and Tommy were going along too. We all got in the car and were going up Fifth Avenue. I said, "Where are we going?" My dad said, "You'll see in a minute or so." We kept on driving until we got to the big house where I had gotten Peaceful. My dad turned in at the big house and stopped the car, the said, "Let's get out and look around a little."

We all got out of the car, even my mother leaving my baby bother on the seat, and walked into the yard. There stood the man that owned the place and he said to wait a minute and he would get the dogs. He went over to the kennel and opened the gate. The dogs all thought it was parade day and all came marching out for inspection. One of the smaller dogs, just a pup yet, I guess, came right over to me where I was sitting on the grass. She just lay down beside me without any further barking, or dancing around, or any thing. She just lay on her tummy with her hind legs folded at the knees, up beside her and her front paws out in front of her. She seemed all ready to get a running jump-start on the very next thing that moved, and she had four white paws on her just like Peaceful used to have.

I petted her and she seemed to like that enough. My dad said, "Do you like the dog?" I said, "Sure I do. But what will you use to pay for her?" My dad replied, "I'll use the money that the man gave me last night for your first dog". I said, "OK, I guess". With that the guy came over to my dad and said, "Let's go get the paper work done and two of them went inside the office. My mom came over to me and said, "She looks almost as good as Peaceful." "We'll just have to wait and see about that part," I said. Then my dad came out, all smiles and said, "Let's go." We all got back in with my baby brother and the dog. Dad backed the car into the parking area and headed out to the street and on Fifth Avenue for the ride home again.

It was hard to get used to the new dog. I kept thinking about all the things that Peaceful used to do. Like just now, I had to call the new dog to get her into the car. Peaceful would just get in the car as if she owned it. Yet there was so much this new dog had going for her. She had the same coloring, the same feet and it seemed, the same temperament that Peaceful had. I thought that in a week or two, I would get used to having her around. I might even get to like her a little. I said to my father, "How much did you pay for this dog anyhow?" He said, "Don't worry your little head about that. Suffice it to say that I used the money the guy had paid me last night for his wife running down Peaceful."

When we got back to the popshop my mom got out first and took my baby brother with her. My dad got out and said, "Aren't you coming?" I got out of the car and the new dog came along with me.

That was a little surprising, so I just walked away and kept going around the popshop building. She came along just as if she was supposed to. I continued to walk around the popshop building. She came along with me right at my heel and never missed a step. I tried running away from her and she wouldn't let me do that either. She just stuck with me all the time, not missing a step. So I stopped and bent down to pet her a little and talk to her very gently. I scratched her behind the ears and petted even more. She seemed to like that a lot. So I kept it up for a little while.

I went for a walk again. This time I went down the little lane that ran past the lumberyard and past the telephone poles that were stored for the phone company. I kept going until I was down near the frog pond. All of a sudden the dog perked up her ears and her head, and looked all around herself. It made me wonder what she had heard. She stopped in the lane and cocked her head over to one side with her ears standing up listening. She had heard something up ahead that caught her interest it seems. But what it was I couldn't figure it out at all.

Just ahead was the frog pond that we liked to go to so much. When we got there the dog started to go on its own. She kept looking at the frog pond for all she was worth and started to go around the whole pond, all the time looking at the frog pond. I couldn't, for the life of me, figure out why she was paying so much attention to the pond. Was it the water? Was it the tadpoles in the water? I couldn't tell what it was. Then she stepped into the water on the far side of the pond, and suddenly all the croaking noise stopped, just as if someone had pulled a switch. She lifted her head and looked at me as if to say, "Where did you put the noise? What can I do now?"

Just then a frog jumped out in front of her and she jumped about three feet in the air in surprise. She backed out of the pond and looked again at the pond wondering what was going on in it. What were these animals that were making all the noise? What makes them stop making the noise when I get close to the water? Were they afraid of a poor little puppy dog, she seemed to say. For an immediate answer all the frogs started croaking again and she jumped back from the pond and then came running over to me. God love her for that. In that moment we became fast friends and she put her front paws up on my leg, stretched out her neck and gave me a big face washing with her tongue. Man, was I ever happy about that! It made my day that's for sure. I just knew that no mater what came, I would always need her and love her.

With that I went around the pond looking for a nice, big frog. I saw one only a little ways down the pond and went over and pounced on it. Lucky for me I caught it just as it was getting ready to jump away. I took the frog over to the dog to show the frog to the dog. I talked to the dog very quietly and tried to tell her that the frog had a life here in the frog pond too. We weren't supposed to make a lot of trouble for the frogs. The frogs were here for our enjoyment just like dogs and people were. The dog kind of looked up at me and kind of said, "OK If that is what you want."

I didn't pursue it any farther. I set the frog down on the ground in front of the dog and stood back and just watched as the dog bent her head down to the frog and smelled it and then gave it a big tongue licking too. The frog looked around then finally turned to me and let out a croak. That told me that all the other animals would be safe when this dog was around. I took that for gospel sure.

I decided to go home then and started out for the popshop with the dog right at my heel. We were going along just fine. The dog was walking with her head up and was looking around at all the sights along the way. This was quite different from our walk down to the pond earlier when she had her head down all the way to the frog pond. I think she was getting on to my way of life, and I liked that part a great deal.

There wasn't much sense in having a dog, or any other animal, that you would always be at odds with, I thought. We came up to the popshop and I started to go around the building. The dog just followed me but had her head up and was looking around a great deal. When we got around to the front of the building, who do you suppose was waiting for us? It was the same lady that had run over Peaceful.

She wanted to know where I had been and what I had been doing. I told her that I had taken the new dog for a walk down to the frog pond and back. She got very interested when I said "the new dog". She said that the new dog looked just like the old one. I said, "Yes, she sure does. And she behaves in much the same ways that Peaceful did too." I said. She said, "Are you happy now?" Then I said, "No, I'm not real happy now. Just come with me and I'll tell you why I'm not real happy now." I went over to the place where we had buried Peaceful and the lady came with me. I told her that this was the spot where we had buried poor Peaceful, and I would have to get a mower to cut the grass around the grave. She asked again what name I had given the dog. I said it was "Peaceful". The lady said thank you. Then she said that she had to leave. "Thank you for coming. It means so much to me," I said.

I went over to the popshop door and went inside. The dog came too. We went up the stairs to the apartment and went in. My mom wanted to know whom I was talking to out in front of the building. When I told her that it was the lady that had run over Peaceful and she was very surprised. She wanted to know what the lady wanted. I said, "I don't really know. Except that she wanted to know what the dogs name was that she had run down." "Well, did you tell her?" my mom wanted to know. "Yes," I said. "But she didn't say why she wanted to know." Then I said to my mom, "You know that we need a lawn mower to cut the grass out front by Peaceful." She said, "Maybe you can cut it with the scythe just as easy as with a mower." I said, "Maybe so. But not for very long."

We didn't say any more about it until lunchtime when my father came home. We were all seated down eating when my mom gave me a kick under the table and pointed outside to the front of the building. So I piped up with, "You know we need a mower to cut the grass out in front with." My dad said, a little annoyed at me, "Just what the heck do we need with a mower for?" "To cut the grass for Peaceful, out in front of the building." I said. My dad hemmed and hawed about that for a few minutes and then said, "We could get a mower if I used it every week to cut the grass." I was pretty happy with that and said, "I'll cut the grass every week if you think it needs it." My mom said, "That means that you have to be here every week, and can't be out at the farm or someplace else either." "Well alright." I said, rather dejectedly.

Anyhow that's how my chore of cutting the grass got started. That's why I didn't get to go to the farm as much anymore. Then I figured out that mowing grass wouldn't take very long and I could do it early on the mornings of the go-to-the-farm days. So that's exactly what I did. I got up early on Saturdays and went out to cut the grass on top of Peaceful's grave. This didn't go along for too long a time though, and all of a sudden one day the woman that ran Peaceful down was back. She wanted to see the grave again. I said to her, "Go ahead and look all you want. I will just tag along if I may." She went over and looked and kind of hummed along. Then she said, "I'd like to see your mother for a minute or so."

That meant that she would have to go into the apartment because of my baby brother. So I said, "Go ahead." She went into the apartment and stayed about a half an hour and then she came out and started to go up the street without saying a word to me. I should care! I went on cutting the grass as nice as I could and then stopped for a rest. After about another hour or so a big truck drove in with "Monuments" painted on its door. I couldn't figure out what it was doing here. When the driver got out he came over to me and said, "Are you the McGraw boy?" I said, "Yes, I am." Then he said, "Where do you want me to put it?" Well that left me in a lurch to say the very least.

"Put what?" I stammered. "The stone, of course." the man said. I said, "You had better go and ask my mom about the stone."

Over to the apartment he went and he went up stairs too. I could hear him talking all the way out here in the yard. He said that the other lady had bought the stone about a month before. Then she had it carved into the shape of a dog lying down with its rear legs underneath and folded up along side her body and her forelegs folded and sticking out in front of her. Her head was up looking ahead and her ears were pointed too. With that my mom said, "Just ask the boy out in the yard where Peaceful's grave is and he will show you."

The man came out again to me and said, "Where is Peaceful's grave, please?" So I said, "Come with me a minute and I'll show you." The two of us walked over to the gravesite, and I said, "Right here." The man then said, "Watch out, because I'm going to back the truck into here to unload." He got back up in the truck and began backing it up. He stopped when he got to the grave. Then he got out of the truck and came to the back end. He opened the back doors on the truck, got up inside the truck and was lifting something heavy. I couldn't see what it was that he was lifting so I just waited for a couple of more minutes until he got to the back doors.

He put down whatever he was carrying and asked, "Where's the head of the grave?" I said, "Its right over here." With that exchange, he lifted the object from the truck and set it down at the head of the grave. Then I could see right away what it was. It was a headstone for the grave. There was a perfect rendition of my old dog Peaceful lying on her stomach with her head up and ears pointed straight up. I couldn't do anything but cry. I said to the guy, "Who ordered this headstone?" All he would say was, "The lady who ran over the dog." He got back into the truck and began to drive off. Soon he was gone and I was left there crying. With that I went over to the new headstone and ran my hand over it.

It was a nice headstone, well done, and good to look at too. It was just a perfect picture of the dog Peaceful. I said thank you to the lady even if I didn't know her name, or where she was at the moment. Pretty quick my mom came down from the apartment and wanted to know what I thought. I said that the lady was pretty nice to give me the headstone, and that my mom should call her up and thank her for me. She said that she would do that this afternoon. With that she turned to go back up to the apartment and I followed her as did my dog. When we got upstairs I went to my room and lay down. My dog came in with me and sat down. She kept looking up at me and whining some. I finally got the idea that maybe she wanted to get up on the bed with me. I said, "Come up here dog." and she did just that. She didn't even back off to get a run at the bed. She just made it from a standing position with no run at it at all.

There were the two of us up on the bed with me petting the dog, and her liking the petting as she lay down beside me. When my mom called me for lunch she said, "You haven't gone to the farm and why not." I said, "Because no one had stopped for me. Besides, I don't think it is such a good idea just yet anyhow." We sat down for lunch with my new dog on the floor by my chair. When I had finished eating I waited for my mom to get done and then we left the table together. My dog hadn't eaten yet so I got some dog food out for her and put it in her metal dish on the floor. She went at it with both ears just flying in the air.

The problem of a name for the dog was still there and I had to think of one pretty soon or go on calling her "dog" all the time. But not yet, I was sill thinking of Peaceful all the time. I thought that I had Peaceful out of my mind pretty much, and then the driver that came this morning reminded me of her once again. Oh well, I missed Peaceful so much, but I had a new dog to keep me company and very good company she was too. Again I thought, "What shall I call her?" All kinds of names went though my mind, and none of them fit her at all. I kept on with the naming process right after lunch but I didn't make any progress at all.

After helping my mom with the dishes I went down stairs and outside again. It didn't seem that a name was possible for the dog, but I just couldn't keep calling her "dog". Time just seemed to fly by us in the afternoon and the first thing I know it was suppertime again. My dad wanted to know what I had been doing all day. I told him about the headstone for Peaceful and trying all afternoon to think of a name for the new dog. I told him about our sojourn to the frog pond and our meeting the frog and all. I told him how my new dog seemed to like the new headstone for Peaceful, too.

I had decided that today was the day to name the new dog, come what may. So I began to think about names in earnest. By gosh! That was it. "Headstone", I'd call her. I went back inside and up the stairs to the apartment. All the while I kept saying the name to myself in my head. When I got the top of the stairs I decided that that wasn't the name I should use. There's got to be another name that I could use. There's just got to be! So I thought and thought some more. I could call her "Chocolate" but that didn't sound right at all. I needed something more personal to name the dog. There just had to be another word to describe her in everyday life. I thought and thought about it and pretty soon I thought that I couldn't think of anything that just fit her. I took her for walk up on McKinley Street. She seemed to be all in favor of the walk and was following nicely at my heel. As we passed Jimmy's house I heard Jimmy call out a "Hello", and we stopped our walk to visit with Jimmy.

I told him about the frog at the frog pond and he said that he wasn't surprised at all. He had been down to the frog pond just the other day and had played with some of the frogs. Maybe that's why the frog had been so friendly to me. The dog and I went on our way up the street to Fourth Avenue and there crossed McKinley Street. We walked down the other side of the street toward Fifth Avenue. There were some dogs on that side of McKinley Street but none came out to meet us and announce our arrival in barking tones. We just kept going down that side of McKinley Street until we got back to 5th Avenue.

At that corner we turned south to go back over to the popshop. After looking both ways for traffic we started across McKinley Street and continued to go south on Fifth Avenue. We got back to the little patch of grass where Peaceful lay, and I sat down to rest a little. Then all of a sudden the name "Brownie" came to mind. Now why in the devil hadn't I thought of it earlier? I couldn't explain it at all. That's the name that I'll use for dog from here on I decided. There's no time like the present I said, and turned to my new dog and tried it out on her. She seemed reluctant come over to me when I first used the name on her. But, I thought, given more time, she would respond to the name.

We went inside and up to the apartment where my mom was playing with my brother. I went over to her and said, "Meet my new friend Brownie". My mother said, "Well you've finally come up with a name. I was wondering why it took you so long." "I just couldn't think of a name until I got done with our little stroll up McKinley Street," I said. "She doesn't seem to like the name very much either," I added. "Oh but she'll get used to the name inside of a week I'll bet." I said. "Well, you're on," said my mom, "you just wait and see if I'm not right." Just about then I could have waited for six weeks to see who was right or not.

Wait, Wait, Wait

The very next Saturday I was out of bed before seven o'clock and down the apartment stairs to the garage area. I got the new mower out of the garage and took it over to the grassy area to mow the grass. It was harder than I had thought it would be. I kept at it and soon it seemed to get a little easier for me. In about an hour I had the mowing all done, and then took the mower back to the garage. The truck drivers were here and giving each other a hand loading his pop and beer onto the trucks. In about another hour the trucks were loaded and each began to leave on each of their routes for the day.

I went up the stairs to the apartment and sat down at the table all ready for breakfast. My mom came in and said, "Where have you been already today?" I said, "I cut the grass, and it's all done for another week". "Well," she said, "Will miracles never cease? You were out mowing the grass and I didn't have to push you to do it. I swear I think the world's coming to an end." With that she got me some breakfast, and told me to eat it all. I did too, while Brownie sat and looked at me as if I were eating the last meal and she was left out of the process. Well no one wanted to leave her out of the meal at all. So I got down from the table and got her some dog food too. Then I got back up on my chair and we had us a race to see which of us could finish first. As things turned out, Brownie was done first and I was left to bring up the rear.

When our breakfasts were done I said to my mom, "I wonder if Grandpa will stop for me this morning or not". She said, "Don't worry about it. I think he'll just stop here after the barber shop." I said, "Well, I'd better go downstairs and wait for him then." Out of the chair I jumped, said, "Come on Brownie", to the dog and lit out down the stairs and out the front door. I went over to the grassy area to wait. I didn't have to wait long, only about two hours or so. Wait, wait, Wait! Up drives Grandpa in the coupe and stopped. Then he said, "Do you want to go out to the farm today?" "Well sure", I replied. "Well you just wait here until after lunch and I'll be back for you then," he said.

There I was waiting once again for all the good things to happen. Just when I was ready, everyone else said to wait for a while. While Grandpa drove away I went to look for a small piece of rope that I could use to tie Brownie to the seat with. I finally came up with just the right length of rope and left it in the grass to wait for Grandpa to come back. Seems like that is all I get to do nowadays was to wait for somebody else to get done doing what ever they were doing to get to do my thing.

Anyway, I said to Brownie, "Let's go up stairs and play with the kid a little." Up the stairs and into the apartment we went. My mom wanted to know if I was going to the farm or not. I said that I would be going as soon as Grandpa got back. That could be as early as this afternoon, if I knew my Grandpa. In the meantime I could play with my baby brother if it was all right with her. She said, "He is getting ready for his morning nap right now. So could you wait until after lunch time?" I said, "Sure, anything you want, mom." I went back down the stairs again and outside.

Brownie and I went to Peaceful's gravesite and sat down on the grass. It was a good thing that I had cut it all this morning to say the least. I thought about taking a stroll down to the frog pond again but decided not to because I didn't know when Grandpa would be back to pick me up. I just lay down on my back and called for Brownie to come over to me. She came right over and lay down beside me. I just started petting her and scratching her behind the ears. She seemed to like that part more than anything and I kept on scratching her until I thought she was asleep after about thirty minutes or so.

I tried to get up then and found that she wasn't asleep at all; she was just faking it a little bit. Pretty soon my Grandpa came driving into the yard. He still had on his town clothes and asked if I still wanted to go the farm. I said, "I sure do Grandpa. When are you leaving?" He said, "Right after I change my clothes. In about an hour I'll be back to pick you up." Then he drove off for the store and a change of clothes. Brownie was all ears during this conversation and seemed very interested in the subject. I actually believe that she had understood every word between Grandpa and me.

In about another two hours my Grandpa came driving into the yard again. I shouted a goodbye to my mom and got in the car. Brownie came along with me and was looking for a place to sit I guess. I took her up on my lap so that she could see a little and we settled in for the ride to the farm. Grandpa said, "Are you ok?" "Yes, we are Grandpa." I said. Then we were driving down the Brooklyn Road headed for the highway out of town.

When we got out to the highway Grandpa said, "I've got to make one stop first before we can go to the farm." "That's fine," I said. He kept driving along the highway past the road to the farm and I got curious about where we were going. So to was Brownie curious, with looks in all directions at once it seemed to me. But that was ok with me as long as she didn't try to get out of the car. Soon, we were coming into Chisholm and then she got real curious. It seems the new surroundings made a hit with her as well as with me. I hadn't been over here to Chisholm for quite some time.

We were just riding along when Grandpa said, "Where is Third Street anyhow?" I said, "Turn left at the O'Neil hotel, and we'll find it pretty soon." "That's where highway 73 turns North I think." He said. Sure enough highway 73 turned north at the O'Neil hotel and we did too. We were just riding along reading the street signs when my Grandpa said, "Here it is." Then he turned onto 3rd Street and was driving along fairly slow looking at the house numbers. Then he suddenly said, "Here it is" and stopped the car. When he got out of the car, Brownie thought that she should get out too. I said, "No" to her and she stopped right away what she was doing and came over to me to lie down again.

Grandpa had gone into the house and we were just sitting there waiting for him to come out again. In about a half hour or so he came out of the house and got back in the car with us. Then he started the car and we went to the corner and turned right to get back to the main street. Once there, we turned left this time and we rode down the hill on Main Street. We were on the dike road that went across the lake. This was a first for me and I kept looking at the sides of the road to see if they would give out and slide us down into the lake. We made it fine without even an inclination of lake water. We got up the hill on the other side of the lake and continued on to the City of Frazier. Just past Frazier we came to the cut off highway that ran through Wilpen and down to Buddy's Tavern on the Iron Junction highway.

Brownie was standing up with her front feet on the armrest of the side window on my side. She seemed to like what she was seeing with all the trees and such going by. I said to her that pretty soon we would get out of the car when we got down to the farm. We were going past Wilpen over the railroad tracks and there was a train going underneath us. Brownie seemed to be very curious about the train and strained to get away from me to see more of it. But by then we were down to the trace that led to the farm, and by then it was too late to see the train any more. We turned onto the trace and started to go around the little lake that sat there. We could see all the places that the crew had trouble holding the new house upright in their passing. My Grandpa said, "Keep a sharp eye out for your deer, now Joey."

I was doing just that and said, "I haven't seen her yet, Grandpa." I kept on watching behind every tree and bush, but had no luck at all. We came to the top of the hill on the trace just past the county road that goes by the farm pasture. Then down the hill we went to the gate to the farm. I got out to open the gate to the farm. Brownie wanted to come with me but I said, "No" to her, and she stayed right in the car waiting for me. I got back in the car I said to Grandpa, "Why don't you leave us off here and we can walk back to the buildings". He said, "OK". Brownie and I got out of the car and started walking the rest of the way. Brownie stayed right with me with her head up and was looking all about her every minute of our little walk.

We got up to the little hill that the new house had come up and Brownie had her nose going 90 miles an hour. She stopped and looked around for a minute or so. I was just watching her every move. She just stood there with her nose going, looking around and turning around, trying to see what she had smelled. Then as if she was following directions she went over to the cage that I had had the deer and rabbit in. Well that was a time to be smelling away if ever there was one. I asked Brownie what she had smelled and she just looked at me as if I were stupid or something. Can't you tell what was here before? She seemed to say. I said, "Yes I know what was here before, Brownie." Then she seemed to take it all for granted, and just mused along with her head held high.

With that I walked down the hill to the little house and went inside. Brownie was ever attentive to my every move and came along with me. She went over and smelled my bed stuff and looked pleased about that move. Then she came over to me and looked back at the bed on the floor just as if to say, "Did you live here too?" I said, "I sure did, Brownie" and went over to a chair and sat down. Brownie came over too and just lay down beside the chair. Gee, but I thought that she was a good friend to have around. Well in all this commotion we hadn't seen Spike at all. I was wondering where he was, but I thought that he would be with Grandpa someplace and we'd get to see him afterward.

Sure enough Spike came running over to the little house to see who was all here. I just sat still and didn't say a word. Spike just came roaring into the little house like he owned it lock, stock, and bootery. He came to a screeching halt the very second that he spotted Brownie. Brownie too was a little startled to see Spike. She got up to her sitting position with her fore legs holding her up. Then Spike came over to her to get to know her a little bit. He just sat down with his fore legs holding him up in front of Brownie and did the nose-to-nose trick with Brownie. In a couple or three minutes they quit the nose-to-nose business and got down to the real meat of the meeting—smelling each other.

With the introductions out of the way we could settle down to a more realistic form of life. They did and soon smelled each other like it was going out of season. When they had gotten done with the smelling routines they just parted and went to find a place to lie down, Spike went over to the area by the stove and Brownie came over where I was and lay down. That meant that all the 'getting to know you' smelling was done for the time being at least.

Brownie At The Farm

This was Brownie's first trip to the farm so I figured that I could expect almost anything at all. I was almost ready for anything to happen, but I wasn't ready for the team. Grandpa had harnessed up the team and was going across the creek with them and we were just standing there by the door to the barn watching for all we were worth. Then the horses came out of the barn and just about trampled us in their endeavor. We got out of the way in a hurry to say the very least. But Brownie had to put her two-cents worth in and started to bark at the team. This scared the team enough so that they started to go on their own. Well I got after Brownie right away and Grandpa held the horses up with the reigns and I put a stop to Brownie with a good scolding. I was sure that she would behave herself around the horses after that.

Grandpa took the team across the creek and over to the hay rake that was parked in front of the chicken coop. Brownie was all eyes at this and watched and watched for the whole time that we stood there in front of the barn. Then I went over to the chicken coop to do my chores. Brownie came right along with me to the chicken coop and right along with me when I entered the coop. This was Brownie's first time to see a chicken, so she entered very quietly with no noise or barking at all. The chickens took one look and thought that Peaceful was back and started right in with climbing onto Brownies back. Then Brownie jumped around and let out a yelp trying to get the chickens off her right away. Well that maneuver scared the dickens right out of the chickens and they flew to other parts of the coop.

It took me a little while of quiet talking to get Brownie calmed down enough to get her to even follow me around to the nests and pick up the eggs. Follow me she did to pick up the eggs and place them into the basket. Then, setting the basket down, I went to get more straw for the nests. When I finally finished that job and the chickens were leaving poor Brownie alone I picked up the basket full of eggs and started to go out the door, with Brownie right behind me, for the little house.

When I got back to the little house I started right in cleaning the eggs. That took a little while and Brownie was just interested as ever. In fact she came over to the table and put her front paws up on the table to see a little better. When she was satisfied about the procedure she got down from the table and went over and lay down by the door.

Today was a pretty good day in the production of eggs, there were about fifteen dozen, so it took me a long while to clean them all. But soon I was ready to start putting them in cartons, so I got out about fifteen cartons and began filling the cartons with the eggs. This operation took about an additional hour to accomplish and Brownie was getting sort of anxious. She was up and walking around a little and making low growling noises as she walked around. The only thing I could do was to talk to her quietly as she walked around to her get settled down again. Soon she was all right again and came over to me and put her chin on my leg. I knew what that move meant, it meant, "Pet Me! Real quick!"

So I put the eggs aside and began to pet her. I scratched her behind the ears until I was tired of scratching and then I quit and just petted her for another half an hour and then went back to putting the eggs in the cartons. When I had gotten all the eggs into the cartons I started in carrying them down to the basement room to keep them cool. Brownie was real curious about that move too and followed me downstairs on each trip that I made.

By the time I had put all the eggs downstairs it was getting to be suppertime. Grandpa came in and began getting supper together for us. It only took a few minutes and it was ready. I got the silverware and dishes out onto the table. Brownie seemed to be quite dejected and I didn't know why. I could see that she was down in the dumps but I couldn't see the reason for her behavior. Try as I might the reason just escaped me. Until after supper was done, and I began to pick up the scraps and put them on her plate. Right then Brownie let out a soft growl and went outside the little house.

I took the plate of scraps outside to her and then I got an education about dogs. She didn't want the scraps from the table. She wanted something else to eat. What it was I was hard pressed to figure out. But I thought that I was being generous with her giving her the table scraps to eat, evidently it wasn't the right food for her. Then I remembered that the guy that had raised her had always given her some dog food to eat. That must the reason for her not wanting to eat the table scraps. So I went and got her some dog food that we had gotten for Spike one time. When she saw the dog food she was all excited and dove right in eating the dog food. Well it appeared as though I had to get some more dog food for her as soon as I could. I made a mental note to ask her former trainer just what brand of dog food he had been giving her before I got her.

I got to wonder when we would go to town again and then I remembered that today was Friday and we would be going tomorrow morning for sure. That wasn't too hard to figure out. Well the very next morning after Grandpa was done with his morning chores early we started off to go to town. I had Brownie with me of course. We stopped at the store and Grandpa got his bath in right away. Then we were off to the barbershop for Grandpa to get his shave and a haircut. When we were done with that we started out in the coupe for other parts of town. We made all the stops at the Italian homes to give them Grandpa's advice on making their wine.

Then we went down to South Hibbing as it was now called and stopped at the Merchants Warehouse. We went in and Grandpa asked if they had any dog biscuits in a big sack. It seems they did have some just lying around and they brought out a sack of the food. I reached into the sack and got a couple of nuggets and turned to give them to Brownie but she even refused to take them in her mouth. Well I couldn't figure that move out at all and said to Grandpa, "We'd better go and ask the guy that raised her about what type of food to try on her." So out to the coupe we went and got in for the ride back up to Hibbing.

When we got there we drove right over to the dog raisers place and parked the car. We walked in to the place and the man came out to see us right away. When he saw Brownie, he was all smiles, and Brownie was excited too. We asked the guy what kind of dog food he fed to the dogs. He told us the brand of dog food we should buy and where to buy it, and he said to wait a minute. Then he went back inside the building and soon came out with a few nuggets of dog food. These he gave to Brownie and she was happy as can be and ate them all down like they were going out of style.

So we got back in the coupe and drove up to Railroad Street to get to the place to buy the dog food at. We found the place right away and stopped out in front of the place. Then we got down from the coupe and went into the building. It was a fine building, all brick and painted up in brown and black. The man there wanted to know what we needed and we said dog food, the kind that the dog raiser man got each time he came in. He went in the back of the place and got a hundred pound sack full of dog food. When Brownie saw that she really got excited and started to run around us and the sack of dog food like there was no tomorrow. Evidently it was the right kind of dog food so we said that we would take it. Grandpa paid the guy for the dog food and we took it out to the coupe. We put it in the rumble seat for the ride back to the farm. Pretty quick we were off to home at the store.

Brownie was real excited about the new dog biscuits and couldn't wait for us to open up the bag. When we did she just sat down and then waited for us to get out some of the dog food. It was strange the way she waited for the dog biscuits. She was all nice and quiet, no barking or jumping around at all. She just sat there quietly waiting for me to get the dog biscuits out and give them to her. When I had got the biscuits out of the sack and gave them to her she immediately started in to eat them and when she had finished three of them, she decided that that had been enough and stopped eating. I was proud as punch to have her for my dog.

Then I wondered if Spike would like them too. Only way to find out was to try them on him when we got back to the farm. So the next morning I fed the dog and tied up the sack of dog biscuits and was ready to go to the farm. But it was Sunday morning and that meant that I had to go to church with my Mom and Dad. So I went up stairs and got cleaned up and put on my Sunday best clothes. Then I just waited for Mom and Dad to get up. I went out to the front room to sit down and wait, and here was aunty Dora sleeping on the couch. Well I couldn't go in there with her sleeping on the couch so I went back into the kitchen and sat down and waited.

Pretty soon my Mom and Dad were up and came in the kitchen looking for some breakfast. They got out some bowls and cereal and the milk from the refrigerator and set a place for me. Then we all ate our breakfast and soon we were ready to go to church. But it was early yet; only nine-thirty and mass didn't start until ten-thirty. So we just sat around and when somebody else came in the kitchen we asked if they wanted to go to church with us. Nobody wanted to go to church with us. That was a little disappointing so we just went down and got in the car. Then we drove up to Superior Street to the church. It was a fine old building with a fine school building along side of it.

We were in church about an hour and a half and Mom said, "Would you like to go to lunch?" "Well," I said, "Sure as the dickens." Away we went to South Hibbing and turned left at Howard

Street. We drove down to the Howard lounge and parked the car. We got out of the car and went into the lounge. Mr. Fotopopulous was right there waiting for us and took us to a booth. He asked my Dad, "Do you think that the booth is all right." My Dad said, "It is just fine, Tom, Thank you." So we sat down and had our lunch.

After lunch we got in the car and drove around the town a little bit. My Mom said, "What do you want to do today?" I said, "Go out to the farm, if I can, to see if Spike would eat the new dog food that Grandpa and I got yesterday." "Well," my Mom said, "you are always going out to the farm. Your dad and I never get to see you at all." I said, "I have to go out to the farm to see if Spike will eat the new biscuits that we bought yesterday." "Well don't forget that school starts in a couple of more weeks and you've got to be ready for that pretty soon," my Mom said.

With that we went back up to the store and I got changed into some clean clothes for the farm. Then I went and got my dog, which was happy to see me, and we got in the car to go to the farm. I got in the car and my Mom got in the driver's seat. My Dad got in the other front seat and we started to go. We drove down the Brooklyn road and out to the highway. We drove down the highway to the Rock-lawn Dairy corner and turned right to get on the road to the farm. We went along just fine with my Mom driving and then we came to the cut-off highway from Chisholm to Buddy's Tavern. We crossed the highway and got us on the trace going to the farm.

My Mom got real nervous about then and stopped the car. My Dad said, "Why did you stop?" Mom said, "Because I don't trust myself out on the trace, you have to drive from here Walter." With that she got out of the car and came around to the passenger side of the car. Dad got out and came over to the driver's side and then they both got into the car.

Pretty quick we were down at the gate to the farm. I got out of the car and opened the gate for the car to get onto the farm. Then I closed the gate and got back into the car and we drove up to the buildings. My dog was all excited to get out of the car when I opened the door. Brownie just jumped out and ran over to the little house doorway and barked our arrival for all to hear.

Grandpa came out of the little house and said, "Hi you people. Come in and have a rest for a bit." Well I got right out of the car and my Mom and Dad did too. I went into the house to see where Grandpa had put the sack of dog food. Sure enough he had put it right inside the door and I went and got several hunks of dog biscuits and took them outside to Spike to see if he would eat them.

At first he was a little hesitant to start eating them, but soon he got one in his mouth and he ate it right down and came up looking for more. This was a little surprising to say the least. "Did this mean that we would have to be feeding him dog food everyday too?" I said. "Well, I guess your guess is as good as mine," my Dad said. With that they got back in the car and headed out of the farm for town. I was on the farm again and happy to be there too.

I was back on the farm and my dog was too. We were both happy about that, especially my dog because now she could be outdoors and roam around as much as she liked, not that she would without me. But that was beside the point. She just wouldn't roam around without me, that's for sure. I decided to go hunting for a little while and got the 22 and some shells. I started to go out the door and Brownie gave a quiet kind of growl. I was at a loss to figure that one out so I said to her, "Brownie you be quiet now or I'll leave you here." Well it seems like that was all it took to really get her attention and she came right over to me and nudged me with her nose.

I decided to go up woodchuck's mound by the railroad tracks and Brownie came right along with me. When we got to the pasture fence I said to Brownie, "Now be quiet from here on. We don't want to scare any chucks that might be out and around." She seemed to understand every word that I spoke. She was very quiet and seemed to know that we were after something but she didn't know what. She kept looking up at me the whole time, just watching me and where we were going.

We got across the pasture fence all right and started up the hill toward the chuck's mound. We had gotten almost up there when I spotted a chuck outside of his hole. I took a sighting on him and shot the 22. When I looked up again he was gone from sight. I couldn't see him anywhere, and Brownie was jumping around to beat the band. I ran up to the chucks mound and didn't see him anywhere until I looked in the hole that was the entrance to the den. There he was just lying there with a small hole in his head all dead as could be. Brownie let out a bark that could be heard all the way back to the buildings. I reached in to the hole and got the dead chuck out and then you should have seen Brownie go nuts over it. She reached over and got the dead chuck in her mouth and started to shake for all she was worth. She then stopped the shaking routine and put the dead chuck down on the ground again.

Well that was all well and good but I wondered what she would do if she was confronted by more than one chuck. So I started to go over to the hill top potato patch. When I had gotten close to there I said to Brownie, "You've got to be quiet now or you'll scare the chucks into hiding in their holes." Then I went quietly to the edge of the potato patch and looked all around. Sure enough there were two chucks in the middle of the patch digging away for all they were worth. So I took a sighting on the two of them when they were lined up one in front of the other, and shot the 22. I looked up and didn't see either of them right away. I walked over to the spot where I had seen them and when I got over there, there were three dead chucks in a row. I hadn't seen the third chuck because he was behind one of the other two.

Well you should have seen the look on Brownies face. It was one of total disbelief the same as was on my face, I guess. But Brownie did her duty and took them each in her mouth and shook them quite well until she thought that they were each dead, and then looked to me for approval of her actions. I said, "OK Brownie, that's a good dog." after each one. She seemed to like all the praise that she was getting and just stood there wagging her tail to beat the band.

At that point I decided to go back to the building area. I took the three dead chucks and started out. I put the three dead chucks into the den holes that were at the other end of the patch. Then I set out to go back to the building area. Well Brownie seemed to like that part well enough and trotted along happily behind me for the trek.

Brownie in town

Brownie was displeased with me I'm afraid, because she used to sleep with me on the farm, she would try to do the same in town. She could never ever be happy with the town arrangements that she had to put up with and wanted always to get in bed with me. She would come to my room with me expecting to get into bed with me and I always had to say no to her when she would try to get up on the bed. She would sit there and whine a little to tell me that she didn't understand why she couldn't be allowed to get into the bed with me.

Well that went on for a little while until she had become used to the sleeping arrangements. Finally one night she just growled at me for not letting her get into bed. Well that was a real surprise when she did that, so one night I patted the bed and said, "Here Brownie", and up she came right away. She was just as happy as could be with me, and the new arrangement, as could she ever be. She burrowed her way under the covers and turned to me as if to say, "Aren't you getting in too?" So I got under the covers too and she was real happy with that move.

She always slept with her back to me. That was very convenient because otherwise I would have her paws in my face when I finally got to sleep. She would snuggle up to me with her back to me to keep warm. She was a good bed partner and she always snuggled up to me with her back to keep me warm. She would always keep her head up until I got under the covers too and if I was taking too long to get under the covers she would always let me know about it with her low bark. If I kept on taking more time to get in bed she would stand up and bark several times at me. Then when I finally would get into bed she would lay down and get settled for the night.

In the mornings I would go downstairs and let her out to do her business. Then I would have to wait for her to come back and let her in again. She was always ready to come back in and if I weren't right at the door to let her in she would set up a howl that could be heard all the way up to the school.

She would like to go down to the frog pond with me. I'd start out going that way and she would start dancing around for all she was worth. She would get all calmed down as soon as we made the turn around the garage and started to head down the lane. She was always ready to greet her friend, the big frog.

One time that I took her down there she got real quiet when we got close to the pond. I didn't know why she had gotten so quiet and kept on going to the pond. When we got to the pond she went over to the lily pad where her friend the frog used to be all the time. Though there was a frog there, she came right back over to me and whimpered a little to tell me that she hadn't found her frog. Well that was a real surprise because the frog was always there and liked to have Brownie come over to see her. The only thing that I could think of was that someone else had been to the frog pond and had caught the frog and taken it with them.

Well Brownie was upset to say the least, and I don't blame her a bit either. After all the two of them had become such good friends, and Brownie would always show her love for the frog by barking and carrying on so much. But leave it to Brownie and pretty soon she got looking toward the houses up the lane a little way. I got to wondering about that and said to her, "Well let's go and see if we can find the frog." So off we went up the lane, past the telephone poles with Brownie leading the way. She had her head up and smelled the air all the way up the lane. When she got up to the garage for the popshop across from Erickson's back gate she stopped as if she couldn't smell any more.

Then it became apparent that the trucks had just been there and their exhaust was covering up whatever scent there was remaining. This was disappointing to say the least. I kept going up the front of Erickson's Lumber Yard and pretty quick Brownie was all happy again smelling away like it was going out of style. She kept me going on past the lumberyard to the alley that ran down McKinley Street. Then she turned in at the Petroni house and went right up to the door.

Well Jimmy was at home and came over to the door. When he saw that it was me, he said for me to come in, which I did. Then he asked what I wanted and I had to tell him that he had our friend the frog. Well that took Jimmy aback. "How did you know that I have the frog?" he said. I told him. "That frog is my dog's friend, and she smelled the frog all the way up here from the frog pond." "Well I didn't know that," Jimmy said, "Why didn't you tell me before I caught the frog?" "Well," I said, "Why didn't you tell me you were going to catch the frog?" I asked Jimmy.

"To tell you the truth I didn't know myself until the time came. Then I just decided to catch it." I said to him, "Where is the frog now?" Jimmy said, "I have him right here in the house. Just a minute and I'll get him for you." With that he went back inside the house for a minute and was soon back to the porch with the frog. Well you could have beaten me over the head after that news; I figured that the poor frog was long since dead and we would never ever see it again. But thanks to Jimmies love of animals it was still alive and croaking

Well Brownie was just ecstatic when she saw the frog in Jimmies hand. She let out a small bark and the frog turned around and saw Brownie and let out a croak that would top all other croaks in the frog pond for sure. Brownie bent over and put her head down by the frog and the two of them were having the best time getting acquainted again. When Jimmy saw this he couldn't believe his eyes and he said, "Since when does a dog stop killing a frog?" "Since the two of them became fast friends." I said. I went on to tell Jimmy about the first time that I had taken Brownie to the frog pond and how the two of them became fast friends.

Jimmy said, "Well if it means that much to the dog, you can take the frog with you if you want." Then I said, "Thanks an awful lot, Jimmy. That's awful nice of you. What were you going to do with the frog anyhow?" "Just going to keep it here at the house is all. But I can always get another frog" he said. "Well why don't you take the frog back to the pond and turn it loose again?" I said. "OK I will right after lunch," he replied. "OK then do it, please," I said.

Well that was a big load off my mind for sure and I suppose the Brownie felt the same way. We didn't have anything else planned for the day so we left and went back to the popshop. When we got there I went and got the mower out of the garage and began to cut the grass in the front area and Brownie just lay down to watch all the proceedings. It didn't take me too long to cut the grass and when I was done I put the mower back in the garage. Then I came back to play with Brownie again.

It was pretty quick lunchtime and Brownie was getting hungry as I was too. So I went over to the building and got out three dog biscuits for Brownie. I gave the biscuits to Brownie and sat down on the grass to wait for my Mom to call me in for lunch. It was only a couple of more minutes and she called me in. Brownie and I went right in and up the stairs. I got cleaned up for the lunch, and Brownie laid down right behind my chair.

After lunch I got the dishes together for my Mom and said, "I think I'll go up to the ball field to see if anybody is playing ball today." So Brownie and I went down the stairs and outside. Then we went across the Brooklyn Road and up the hill to the ballpark. As luck would have it, there were a bunch of guys, all older than me playing ball. So I just sat down to watch them for a little while. Seems like they were a man short on one side and they asked me to play. I said, "Sure I'd like to play." They said, "OK. Go out to the outfield and take a glove." Out to the outfield I went and I had to tell Brownie to stay there in the dugout to wait for me. She didn't like that part a bit and tried her best to come out to the outfield where I was going.

Well the next two guys up hit a fly ball apiece and the other fielders caught both balls putting the side out. Our team went into the dugout and the captain said that I was the next man up. So I got up and walked out to the batter's box. Brownie figured that she was going to bat too, I guess, because she trotted out with me. So I had to tell her, "No! You're staying back here in the dugout and liking it." Well that went over like a lead balloon but she stayed in the dugout. I went out to the batter's box and swung real hard at the next pitch and I hit it. The ball sailed over everyone's head in the outfield and came down out in the grass someplace beyond the reach of the fielders. When I rounded third base and was coming home here comes Brownie running lickety split out to me.

Well, I and all the other guys, was elected to look for the ball. It reminded me so much of the time that I had hit another ball with Peaceful there watching me. This time though one of the other guys found the ball almost right away. They all wanted to know how I got such a good hit on the ball and I said, "I get good hits because of my dog." They all chimed in, "Tell me another one will you."

After the game was over Brownie and I headed back to the pop-shop. The guys all trooped after us and said, "Do you live here?" "Yes, I do." I answered. "This is the place that they make pop in isn't it?" they asked. I said, "Yes this is the place where we make the pop." Then they all wanted to know if they could come inside and see the pop being made. "What do you think Brownie? Should I take them inside?" Brownie gave a short, kind of quiet bark and I took that to mean, "OK!" So inside we all went, and when we got in the small office I said to them, "Now please keep the talk down a little bit when we're going through the shop."

It was the second day that Roy was making Whistle orange and he was kind of surprised by all the onlookers. He explained the workings of the various machine to them and then said, "Would you like a bottle of pop now?" "Sure we would." They all said together. So Roy took the bottles right off the line as they were filled and capped and they all had a bottle of pop. Brownie kept watching each of the guys and when they were done with the pop she went over to the bottle washing machine and stood there while each guy came over and put their bottle in the front of the machine to be washed again.

When they were all done I took them out of the building by way of the loading platform. Brownie thought that that was real nice and waited inside till the last of the boys had gone out. Then it was time for her to go out also but not without me. She came over to me and put her head behind my leg and gave me a little nudge to go out also. Well, what could I do but go out with all that help?

Brownie had gotten to know most of the guys during the ball game and went to each one and got petted a little, which she liked an awful lot. The guys all said that I could play with them anytime which I thought was awful nice of them. To be a member of their gang was a complement indeed. I took that to mean that a young guy like myself could be a member of an older bunch of guys club. I was happy as could be about that. Maybe, I thought, just maybe it was the start of the end to all the gangs that had mushroomed up over the past year or so. If it was, I was happy about that and Brownie seemed happy too.

One afternoon I was out playing with the bat and ball and decided to go up to the ballpark. Brownie was all ready to go up there too and quietly got behind me for the walk over there. When we got out to the Brooklyn Road I made sure that I looked both ways to check for oncoming cars and when the road was clear I ran across the road. Brownie came right along with me and ran across the road too when I did. You can't be too careful about the traffic especially since there was a curve in the road just above the alleyway where we were.

I always was very vigilant about the traffic and I tried to teach Brownie a little bit about it too. She was very receptive to my teaching her about the traffic and always looked both ways on her own even when I was with her. When we got across the road and started up the hill to get to the ballpark Brownie was right with me, and when we got up to the ball field she went right over to the dugout to her assigned position. Well, I called her back and explained that there weren't any other boys here today so she could be with me all the time. She seemed to like that quite well and stayed right with me.

Then I started tossing the ball up in the air and hitting it when it came down. The first few times that I hit the ball, Brownie was up and at them ready to go get the ball. Then I got a good hit on the ball and it sailed quite high and beyond the outfield and came down some place in the grass past the outfield. Well Brownie took right off to get the ball and she was gone for about a quarter of an hour and then she came back to the out field area and looked at me rather quizzically. "Where did you hit the ball to?" she seemed to say. I put the bat down and ran out to where she was.

We looked around together and didn't find the ball. I went down the hill looking for the ball thinking that it had gone down farther and didn't find it. Brownie was looking all over the place too and couldn't find it either. Well what do you think about that? With both of us looking as hard as we could we weren't finding the ball. There has got to be a reason I said. The ball didn't just disappear. Brownie was going all over with her nose going faster than ever too. I got to thinking that maybe the ball wasn't here where we were looking.

Maybe it was still up by the outfield. I went back up the hill and started looking around up there in earnest. Brownie had stayed down below and kept looking around. I went around kicking all the clumps of grass. The ball just wasn't around anyplace. This is ridiculous I said to no one in particular. I was about to kick a clump of grass that I was sure I had kicked before when I spotted the ball. I called Brownie and said to her, "I can see the ball." She started to look around even harder than she had been looking down the hill.

Another fifteen minutes had gone by and though she was close to the ball, she didn't find it. She came close couple of times but that was all. I was debating with myself if I should tell her or not, when she suddenly came upon the ball. She let out a loud bark, of success I guess, and went over to scoop up the ball in her teeth. Well, she bent down to the ball with her mouth open ready to bite the ball, and she did just that. She lifted up her head with ball clenched in her teeth and looked over at me with a look of total satisfaction.

She was just happy that she had found the ball at last. She turned around to me and then came over to me and dropped the ball at my feet, as if to say, "Go hit it again." So I did go over to the plate area and started to hit the ball again, but this time I didn't hit the ball quite so hard. It went as far as the outfield area but that is about all. I kept hitting the ball the rest of the afternoon and kept Brownie running her head off finding the ball and bringing it back to me.

It was great fun to have Brownie around all day. She could almost understand the English language and seemed to know what we were talking about all the time. She was always a joy to have around and I dreaded not being with her. She made up the fifth friend that I had that year, and was I ever happy to have her around.

Another time we were in the front yard at the popshop when suddenly she lifted up her head and turned around to be facing the back of the building with her head up and ears at attention. She had heard something back there that interested her. She was standing there kind of listening and from the back of the building came a bark. She immediately went into a defensive position and just waited. In a couple of minutes out comes a little puppy about three months old that came right over to her and went into the smelling routine.

Well Brownie didn't know if she was afoot or horseback. She just left the little puppy sniff her all it wanted to and then after a couple of minutes she began to smell the puppy. When they were all done with the smelling routine they each sat down facing each other and started to do the nose-to-nose routine. This went on for about a half hour. When they were done with this they started to play around with each other. Play they did, kind of rough housing it around the grass, with first Brownie lying down and then the puppy lying down. The two of them were just playing around.

Brownie was with me for many years to come while I grew from a child to a young man.

978-0-595-46237-7
0-595-46237-5

www.ingramcontent.com/pod-product-compliance
Lightning Source LLC
Chambersburg PA
CBHW060457290526
45791CB00001B/164